REMAKING TEAMS

REMAKING TEAMS

The Revolutionary Research-Based Guide That Puts Theory into Practice

Theresa Kline

Jossey-Bass
Pfeiffer

San Francisco

Copyright © 1999 by Jossey-Bass/Pfeiffer
ISBN: 0-7879-4648-6

Library of Congress Cataloging-in-Publication Data

Kline, Theresa.
    Remaking teams: the revolutionary research-based guide that puts theory into practice/
Theresa Kline.
        p. cm.
    Includes bibliographical references and index.
    ISBN 0-7879-4648-6
    1. Teams in the workplace. 2. Organizational effectiveness. 3. Industrial organization. I. Title.
    HD66.K587   1999
    658.4'02—dc21   99-33626

Printed in the United States of America

Published by

Jossey-Bass 350 Sansome Street, 5th Floor
Pfeiffer San Francisco, California 94104–1342
(415) 433–1740; Fax (415) 433–0499
(800) 274–4434; Fax (800) 569–0443

Visit our website at: www.pfeiffer.com

Acquiring Editor: Matthew Holt
Director of Development: Kathleen Dolan Davies
Developmental Editor: Diane Ullius
Senior Production Editor: Pamela Berkman
Manufacturing Supervisor: Becky Carreño
Cover Design: Bruce Lundquist

Printing   10 9 8 7 6 5 4 3 2 1

This book is printed on acid-free, recycled stock that meets or exceeds the minimum GPO and EPA requirements for recycled paper.

This book is dedicated to my mother and mentor,
Frances Babbitt.

CONTENTS

LIST OF FIGURES AND EXHIBITS

Figures

Exhibits

LIST OF TEAM EXERCISES ON DISK

PREFACE

Remaking Teams is a guidebook to assist teams operating in organizational contexts. It provides practical suggestions, a theoretical framework, and substantive research, which combine to form a comprehensive, systematic approach to better team performance.

Teams are a pervasive part of the organizational landscape today. When organizations restructure, one of the most common approaches to work reengineering has been to form workers or groups of workers into teams. The success of those teams, however, is usually far less than most organizations hope for. In addition, small businesses are a fast-growing sector of the economy; they are largely started and staffed by a few expert members. These expert members often do not realize their potential as a team.

Purpose of the Book

Many resources are available regarding teams. However, until now, there has been no book that synthesizes team knowledge across disciplines and models it into a coherent whole, no resource that translates the model into a usable guide for practice, and no resource that is based on high-quality, replicated, empirical research in the practice of how to improve team performance. This book examines the question, "What can be done to make the most of my team's efforts?"

The theory and research-based responses to this question are supplemented with several practical ways to put this knowledge to use, including but not limited to assessment tools for teams, their contexts, and their supervisors; case studies; and exercises.

You should read this book if:

- You are a member of a team that is having difficulty performing or is performing at less than capacity.
- You are going to set up a team-based organization and want to do it right from the start.
- You want to maintain the success of your team.
- You want a synthesis of the latest research that has a direct application to working teams.

Making teams effective is an essential part of organizational life. Many organizations jumped on the team bandwagon in the early 1990s in the hopes of improving productivity, minimizing the adverse effects of downsizing, and generally replacing layers of middle managers with self-governing groups of workers. However, many organizations that I have worked with in the past few years have become increasingly frustrated with teams. One client recently told me that she did not even want to use the word to describe the work groups that were being created in her workplace, a large telecommunications organization.

Why is this happening? The reasons are that employers have not seen the improvements expected from using a team-based approach to building their organizations, and employees have come to suspect that being called a member of a "team" is tantamount to allowing the organization to dump more work on them.

I find these responses both disheartening and understandable. From a researcher's perspective, I see tremendous opportunities to assist teams in being successful. From a practitioner's perspective, I have observed a willingness on the part of both employers and employees to try to make their teams successful. There are numerous high-quality studies on which organizations can confidently base team initiatives. There also are numerous studies demonstrating what does not work to improve team performance. I have observed employees being "teamed" when no team is needed to do their jobs. In other situations, teams are created without the requisite support for ensuring their success. Things like this don't have to happen.

I am convinced that teams can succeed. I am also convinced that a team-based approach to organization building takes thought, time, and effort. The purpose of this book is to highlight what is known about making teams successful, and then to make that knowledge available in a systematic, concise, usable manner.

Book Plan and Organization

Chapter One introduces the model that will be explained in detail in the rest of the book: the Team Performance Model. This chapter is the road map for the rest of the book. It also provides a brief historical context in which to place current team theory and practice. Although this section is not a must-read for those who want to get to the meat of the book, it is not overly technical and it is useful—especially for those who have taken team-building courses and wondered about the origins of some of the exercises. I have provided the same material in lectures to several dozen audiences, and the most common responses are surprise and laughter.

Chapter Two takes on the challenge of explaining what is meant by various types of teams. It helps grapple with the fundamental question, "What is a team anyway?" The latest research suggests that crews, task forces, and standing teams are *not* all the same. Although there are some common necessities for the functioning of all teams, the different types require somewhat different approaches to make each highly effective in its particular circumstances.

Chapter Three begins the detailed discussion of the model with the first set of variables deemed to be necessary but not sufficient for success: resources! Not too surprisingly, if teams have too few resources with which to accomplish their work, they do not perform well. The question "How can a determination of the needed resources be accomplished?" is dealt with as an exercise.

Chapter Four speaks to variables in the organizational context that are vital for the success of teams. These include the organization's systems, policies, procedures, and leaders. Assessment tools are provided to give you and your team a sense of how you are doing on these important dimensions.

Chapter Five delves more deeply into the team as a unit and the team's characteristics. The most important are goal-setting, role clarity, and team efficacy. Techniques for assessing and improving these aspects of the team are provided.

Chapter Six examines some of the dispositions and characteristics of the team members themselves. The evidence is clear that although these variables are not as important as those discussed previously, they can and do have some effects on team performance. The search for good team players is one that many organizations continue to carry out. This chapter provides some needed information on this critical personnel issue.

Chapters Seven and Eight also have an internal focus in that they examine how a team processes its work. The issues covered are how to structure and organize the work, utilize team member skills, conduct effective team meetings, make team decisions, and manage conflict.

Even though team "outcomes" are extremely important to organizations, surprisingly few team evaluation systems are actually used. Chapters Nine and Ten focus on what is meant by team performance and how to go about measuring such an elusive construct. In addition to measures of team output, these chapters address the satisfaction of team members and viability of the team itself to continue to function effectively. Evaluation instruments are provided in these chapters.

Chapter Eleven provides a brief discussion about how technology is changing the nature of teams. In our information-based, fast-paced economy, it is only natural that teams should be taking advantage of the technology available to them to enhance information flow and interactions—even when the teams are located in different places. But what do we really know about how teams use technology? How can we determine what they actually need by way of technological advances? These are new, exciting, and still-unanswered questions in the domain of team performance.

Chapter Twelve summarizes the book. It reviews the best practices in team performance, addresses issues facing teams in practice, and offers some speculation about the future of team research.

Chapters Two through Eleven each provide an opportunity to put into practice the lessons learned by means of case studies, instruments, guidelines, or other tools. The disk that accompanies *Remaking Teams* will aid readers in this task.

In writing this book, I have been committed to the fundamental principle of ensuring that the reader understands, learns, and uses this material. I hope that you and your team will benefit from it.

Calgary, Alberta, Canada   Theresa Kline
July 1999

ACKNOWLEDGMENTS

Several individuals were instrumental in getting this book to press. The first is Dr. Richard Guzzo. I first heard Dr. Guzzo speak at the annual meeting of the Canadian Psychological Association in 1991. His enthusiasm for team research that focused on the context of teams, rather than on individual differences between team members, struck a chord with me. I also took to heart his admonition that team research needed to be carried out in the working world. I have been engaged in team research in the field ever since.

Next, Linda Martin, an ergonomist by training, carries out her work in team settings. One day she asked me to tell her what I knew about team effectiveness. Over a very long cup of coffee, I described many of the concepts outlined in this book. Linda told me that I needed to write this down so that others could benefit. So I did.

The editorial assistance of Kathleen Dolan Davies and Diane Ullius made this work a substantially "better read" than if I had been left to my own devices. I thank you—and the readers thank you.

I would be completely remiss if I did not thank my research assistants, Helen Gardiner, Michelle MacLeod, Joni-Lynne McGrath, and Yvonne Sell, who helped me collect data over the years. Finally, my thanks to all the team members, team managers, and team coaches who provided not only the data for my research program but all sorts of ideas about how to improve team performance.

THE AUTHOR

Theresa Kline is an associate professor at the University of Calgary. She earned her Ph.D. degree in industrial-organizational psychology in 1990 and has been a faculty member since her appointment to the University of Calgary in 1991. Her research interests include team performance, career development, psychometrics, and decision making.

Kline has published work in *Educational and Psychological Measurement, Organization Development Journal, Human Factors,* and several other journals. She supervises many graduate students in the industrial-organizational psychology program and is also the director of the research unit, Creating Organizational Excellence, which strives to ensure that graduate students are given ample opportunity to put research and theory into practice.

Kline is an active consultant to business and industry in such diverse areas as team performance, organizational stress, strategic change, job satisfaction, and program evaluation. The combination of her field research and consulting work has contributed to an appreciation for the changes affecting almost all organizations today.

CHAPTER ONE

MODELING TEAM PERFORMANCE

For the past many years teams have become increasingly popular as the way organizations accomplish their work. In a recent study, Osterman (1994) states that more than 50 percent of organizations have used teams as part of their reorganizational efforts. The predictions of higher organizational performance using teams, however, have not materialized (for example, Cappelli and others, 1997). Thus, because teams are so prevalent in organizations, and because they don't seem to be working, it is time to reevaluate what we know about teams and how they can be assisted to perform to their potential.

Teams are not a new organizational phenomenon. Their increased prevalence is what is new. For example, Peter Drucker predicted the team phenomenon as far back as 1959: "The new organization is transforming work that was previously confined to individual effort. It does not replace the individual by organization; it makes the individual effective in teamwork" (p. 68). A classic work by Leavitt in 1975 entitled "Suppose We Took Groups Seriously. . . ." foreshadowed the implications of actually making groups rather than individuals the building blocks of the organization. Later, Peters and Waterman (1982) argued that "excellent" companies are those that use the group as the building block of the organization. Sundstrom, DeMeuse, and Futrell (1990) have given examples of how work teams are being used for such diverse functions as production, product development, quality control, and negotiation. Guzzo and Shea (1992) indicated that, more than ever before, organizations are relying on groups to get their work done, as evidenced by the mushrooming number of project teams, focus groups, and quality circles. Nadler and Ancona (1992) reported that within executive offices, team-based organizations are replacing the traditional executive structures. Guzzo (1995a) states, "Teams and teaming have become hot topics, 'almost faddish' in recent years, as organizations have come to rely on team-based arrangements to improve quality, productivity, customer service, and the experience of work for their members" (p. 1).

The Overall Model

With all the indicators of the importance of teams to organizations, it is interesting to note that if an organization wants to move to a team-based personnel system, there are few concise resources to assist it in that endeavor. The model presented in Figure 1.1 summarizes much of the existing research and practice of what actually works in making teams successful. The parts of the model will be described in detail throughout the book.

The construct of *resources* is critical. If the team does not have the necessary physical, financial, and human resources, the work will not get done. The amount of resources an organization is willing to commit to teams is directly related to the

FIGURE 1.1. TEAM PERFORMANCE MODEL.

organizational context. More specifically, the policies and procedures set up to reinforce teams, the support for teams, and the leadership provided to teams are critical in terms of a team's ability to be successful.

The more supportive the organizational context, the more likely the team will be to process its work effectively. In addition, the more supportive the organizational context, the more likely the team will be to develop healthy characteristics. The *team characteristics* of particular importance to team performance are goal clarity, role clarity, and team efficacy. The more healthy the team characteristics are, the more likely the team will be to process its work effectively.

Differences in *individual disposition* between team members moderate the relationship between the team characteristics and how well the team processes its work. That is, very negative team members may negatively influence the work processes of the team, and very positive team members may positively influence the work processes. However, individual team member dispositions do not overcome the variables of the organizational context or team characteristics.

The *work process effectiveness* portion of the model examines how teams actually complete their work. It includes the skills used by team members, the variety of tasks in which the team members engage, the feedback provided to the team, the autonomy of the team, and other work process issues.

How well the team processes its work is directly tied to the outcomes of the team's work. These outcomes are broken into three categories. The first is of primary concern to the organization: *outcome effectiveness,* which focuses on the quality and timeliness of the team's outputs. *Team viability*—the ability of the team to continue working together—is also important. Specifically, how much the team likes working together is important for teams that need to continue to do so; for project-based teams, this outcome is less important. Finally, individual *member satisfaction* should also be of interest to organizations. Team members who like what they do and who find working with their fellow team members a positive experience are more likely to be committed to their teams.

Before beginning the next chapter, which starts to delve into each aspect of the model and how all relate to team performance, the next section of this chapter places the model into a historical context. Teams and groups have been important to working life for a long time. Research into the phenomenon, however, did not begin until the 1930s.

A Brief History of Teams

In the early 1930s, research conducted at the Hawthorne Works of the Western Electric Company in Chicago began to change how researchers understood the nature of work. These famous studies alerted human researchers to the now well-known Hawthorne Effect, a form of bias in which the behavior of participants in experiments is changed from "typical" simply because the participants know that they are in an experiment. The other outcome of this research—and the more pertinent one for the purposes of this book—was that the *social* aspects of the workplace fulfill important human needs (Mayo, 1933; Roethlisberger & Dickson, 1939).

The next significant foreshadowing of the importance of social aspects of work came through a series of projects conducted in the 1950s by the Tavistock Institute on the British coal mines. These studies revealed the importance of intact work groups in organizational performance and helped foster the development of the sociotechnical theory of organizations. The cornerstone of sociotechnical theory is a presumption that groups at work have social as well as technical systems that must be attended to. If changes to one system occur without sufficient attention to the other systems, then performance is likely to be less than optimal (Trist, 1981).

These classical works put the spotlight on the group rather than the individual worker. They are also well grounded in the work context. Although commendable in both regards, these studies, unfortunately, did not provide specific recommendations for organizations when it came to the building, maintenance, and possible repair of teams of workers.

These shortcomings left the door wide open for another stream of research and practice to evolve. By the 1960s, almost all the group research (more than two thousand studies) was taking place in university laboratories; the participants were undergraduate students involved in tasks in which they had no vested interest (McGrath & Altman, 1966). The inability to translate findings from this research into everyday organizational practice is not at all surprising. Why expect otherwise? For example, in a typical research project, teams of five psychology undergraduates work on a task where they have crashed on the moon and have to prioritize the items left from their spacecraft. In contrast, in the world of work, a team might be charged with finding ways to improve customer service at a retail store where employees are young, turnover is high, pay is minimum wage, the shop is unionized, and managers are accountable to stockholders for a quick return on investment. The parallels between these two teams are scant, if any.

In the 1960s and early 1970s, research focused on the personal characteristics of the team members. The impetus for this approach came from Steiner (1972), who emphasized the importance of something he called *process loss*. That is, the *actual productivity* of the team consistently fails to match the *potential productivity* of the team because of process loss factors. These factors were assumed to be located within the team members themselves. Process loss factors examined by researchers were numerous and variable; they included the gender, race, and personality of members as well as communication and group size. Those who subscribe to this theoretical framework use such techniques as personality testing, whitewater rafting trips, and adventure-based learning as primary team-building interventions, based on the premise that if team members know one another's personalities or like one another, they will perform better in the organization. These approaches are alive and thriving in today's marketplace. What they lack, however, is evidence to substantiate their claims of usefulness in making teams more effective (Reddy, 1994).

Another way that process loss has manifested itself in the popular team-building approaches is the notion that teams are developing organisms and that they go through stages of development. The most prominent example of this is Tuckman's (1965) four-stage model of *forming, storming, norming,* and *performing.* During the first three stages the group does not perform, but instead is focused on group conflict resolution. It should be noted that this model resulted from work with therapy, laboratory, or training groups—not real teams in real contexts. But imagine the following situation: The cockpit crew of a 747 boards the plane twenty minutes before takeoff. You are seated in seat 17B, and as the airplane rushes down runway nine you hope like hell that this team is past the storming stage of group development. Stages and personalities aside, there is something about that cockpit crew that enables the members to get the plane off the ground safely even with having just met one another. Teams that act like this are worth examining in detail.

Gersick (1988, 1989) also is dubious about the four-stage model. In her work with project teams, she finds that what she calls *punctuated equilibrium* is the normative model for staged team behavior. Specifically, a project team does not accomplish much up to about the halfway point to completion (this midpoint occurs regardless of the time frame involved). All of a sudden, at this midpoint, there is a flurry of activity, and the team organizes itself in ways that do not resemble Tuckman's model.

Organizations and employees are fed up with interventions based on process loss. These approaches simply have not worked. The time taken away from work from the employees' perspective, as well as the minimal return on training investment from the organization's perspective, have given team training a bad name.

Recent Research Trends

As the 1970s progressed and in the 1980s, team research withered. The effects of the laboratory-based, process loss approaches weren't working in the real world. The research torch lighted by social psychologists in group work was dropped. It was not picked up again until the latter part of the 1980s and into the 1990s. Those who picked it up were the organizational researchers—people who recognized the critical role played in team performance by factors *outside* the team.

The recognition of these variables has caused a resurgence of interest among the research community to do something useful for teams. They are loosely grouped into a category called *contextual variables*. Empirical work by Hackman (1987), Nieva, Fleishman, and Reick (1978), Gladstein (1984), Shea and Guzzo (1987a), and Sundstrom, DeMeuse, and Futrell (1990) all support this perspective. These contextual variables are powerful tools for improving team performance. Organizations using these tools have observed substantial effects in their teams' performance.

These variables have been understudied and underutilized from a practitioner perspective. I believe that one reason why these variables have not been exploited is that they take a lot of "up-front" effort on the organization's part and must be consistently maintained at the system level in order to work appropriately. It is much simpler and cheaper to send employees on a whitewater rafting trip or an adventure-based weekend than it is to change a performance management system to incorporate teams.

The model described here and detailed in the following chapters capitalizes on the best of what we have learned about both team processes and team contexts, with the final goal of improving real team performance in real organizations.

CHAPTER TWO

A TEAM BY ANY OTHER NAME . . .

What is meant by the term *team* when it is used in an organizational context? Whenever I talk about this issue, I always start with a story that quickly homes in on the point of it. The story comes from a landscaper who worked for a large organization with several acres of grounds to tend. For ten years, none of the workers had been in a team—until recently. Now, instead of planting shrubs and getting on with the job, the landscaper was attending team meetings at which nothing was accomplished. He saw no reason to be part of a team—he planted his shrubs, someone else mowed the lawn, someone else sprayed the trees, and so on.

This anecdote highlights the need to understand the problem that is to be solved by moving to a team-based personnel management system. For this landscaper, there was no problem; or if there was, it was not clear to him. Perhaps instead of being made a "team" that group of employees should have been called simply the "Landscape Department" and continued to work as individuals, as they had for the past several decades. Before proceeding to reorganize the organization into teams, the first question that should be answered in the affirmative is this: "Is a team approach the most effective means by which to achieve work improvement?"

Not all organizations should use teams to get their work accomplished. Before embarking on a team-based route to personnel management, there should be a clear reason for using teams. The answer to at least one of the following questions should be yes before deciding that it will be worth the time and trouble of setting up and running a team:

- Is the task complex enough to need different types of skills as input for its completion?
- Is the task so large that more than one pair of hands is needed to accomplish the work?
- Is there a high degree of interdependency among workers such that a team would facilitate communication and work flow?

Some work units are called teams when, in effect, they are not. A commonly used definition of teams is that they are "distinguishable sets of more than two individuals who interact interdependently and adaptively to achieve specified, shared, and valued objectives" (Morgan and others, 1986, p. 3). It is a disservice to call individual workers a team when they are not. Going back to the landscaper anecdote, the team concept was not a viable one for him or his fellow workers. They were not distinguishable as groups of two or more people, they worked independently rather than interdependently, each person had different goals and objectives, and their work was evaluated on an independent basis. Calling them "a team" was frustrating for them and served no organizational purpose. Furthermore, there was a downside for the workers in being treated as a team: they were now expected to attend team meetings where nothing of "on task" value was being done, and these meetings kept them from actually doing their jobs.

However, teams are appropriate for many types of work and tasks. If a team is indeed appropriate, the next question to ask is, "What *type* of team is appropriate?"

Types of Teams

Are teams, crews, task forces, work groups, and units all the same? The answer seems to be no (for example, Cannon-Bowers, Salas, & Blickensderfer, 1998; McGrath, Berdahl, & Arrow, 1995; Webber, 1998). For team members and team coaches, defining the type of team is essential before starting to think about what needs to be done to make the team more successful.

Setting up effective teams and successful team interventions will quite clearly depend on what is meant by the word team. A common language is helpful in determining team needs. Unfortunately, there is as yet no common way to talk about different types of teams. This situation, however, is changing. In the latter part of the 1990s there has been a concerted effort on the part of several researchers to tackle the task of building a taxonomy of teams. Their work suggests that there are fundamental differences between team types and that it is important to attend to them. This line of research has revealed several common threads in what differentiates team types, including degree of structure of the task, prescriptiveness of the roles of the members, nature of the communication between members, nature of the information exchange between members, and type and degree of sharing of common goals among the members. Depending on where the team falls on these dimensions, there are ramifications for where effort needs to be placed to make the team more effective. Exhibit 2.1 highlights the differences between team types.

Crews: Well-Defined Teams

For the first example, think about a work group that operates under the following conditions: the task is highly structured; roles are highly prescribed; communication links are well defined; need for information exchange is high; and common, usually short-term goals, are shared. This is an example of a type of team with which most people are familiar: cockpit crews, surgical teams, and football teams are all examples. If crews are not as effective as they should be, there are specific reasons for it.

When the type of work they do is examined, it becomes apparent where interventions might be most appropriate. Crews by definition work on highly structured tasks. If the task is ill-structured, the crew can no longer operate effectively. Conversely, if the task is made more structured, the crew will be able to operate better. Therefore, the first thing to examine in a crew situation is the degree of structure of the crew members' tasks.

EXHIBIT 2.1. COMPARING TEAM TYPES.

Type	Task Structure	Role Definition	Communication Links	Information Exchange	Goal Descriptor
Crew	Highly structured	Prescribed	Well defined	High but often implicit	Common, short term
Task Force	Highly unstructured	Loose	Ill defined	High, explicit	Common, both short term and long term
Standing	Multiple/ dynamic	Undifferentiated	As needed	Moderate but continual	Multiple, long term

The second defining feature of a crew is the high degree of specialization and skill level of each crew member. The result is that each crew member knows what the other members are to do and also has some idea of the set of knowledge and skills each member brings to the crew. In a surgical team, for example, the surgeon has a specified role; all the other members of the team know that role and act accordingly. In a flight cockpit crew, the navigator has a prescribed role; the other crew members know what that is and the skills that individual brings to the task at hand. Another feature of a crew is that individual members are easily transported into a different crew. There is very little need for the crew members to become acquainted before beginning their tasks. Clarifying roles for crew members early and unambiguously is essential to their success and therefore a primary consideration when a team is a crew.

One other consideration for effective crew functioning at the individual role level is that crews usually have highly skilled members. Thus, interventions at the crew member level often involve the acquisition of highly trained or very skilled individual members. The more such members populate the crew, the more likely the crew will operate effectively.

Communication between members of a crew is carefully prescribed. Crews usually are hierarchical in that a senior member is ultimately responsible for the accomplishment of the task. As a result, the hierarchy prescribes the flow and type of communication that takes place. Directions and decisions emanate from the senior individual (captain, surgeon, quarterback, and so on), and everyone is expected to toe the line. Any feedback directed toward the senior member is informational but nonsuggestive. Interventions to make crews more effective need to examine closely the communication links between crew members.

Because of how communication works in a crew, the senior member must have access to all pieces of information relevant to the task. Communication structures need to be set up to ensure that this information exchange is smooth, and these structures must be closely adhered to by all crew members if the crew is to operate effectively.

Another characteristic of crews is that information exchange for work flow between members occurs in a highly prescribed fashion. There are very few ways to get an airplane to take off, there are very few ways to take out a gallbladder, and there are very few ways to run a particular offensive football play. The sequence and timing of the tasks of each member are well defined. Only a small degree of freedom is available to crew members to do their tasks differently. Therefore, interventions to improve the work flow for crews would consist of examining whether tasks should be sequenced as they are and how tasks are linked together. In addition, ensuring that all crew members clearly understand the timing and sequencing of tasks is critical. It is difficult to make changes to task routines for crews. Crew members are very used to operating in a certain manner, and it is easy to slip back into old routines after changes have been introduced. As a result, new technology can pose particular problems for crews because they change the timing and sequencing of tasks.

Finally, there is usually little doubt about the expected outcome for crews. Thus, crew members share common goals and the extent to which goals are realized is understood by all parties. Feedback on goal attainment is rapid. Airplanes are expected to take off, fly, and land on time and without any incidents; surgeries are expected to be successful; football games are expected to be won. Therefore, goal-setting interventions for crews are not as important as they are for other types of work groups.

From all of the foregoing it can be seen that a crew approach to building a team is useful under the right conditions. If a task is very well defined, skilled members are readily available, goals are known to be shared among members, and members are comfortable with a hierarchical approach to communication and decision making, then crews are a very efficient means by which to accomplish work. But if these conditions are not met, then a crew approach to team building will not be effective and in fact will have some very counterproductive side effects. For example, if the secretaries who work in a common pool are going to be set up as crews, then senior secretaries will need to be appointed and the other secretaries will have to "follow orders." This approach may not be appropriate for secretarial work.

Task Forces: Teams with a Short-Term Goal

For the second example, think about a work group that operates under the following conditions: the task is highly unstructured, roles are loosely defined, communication links are not defined, need for information exchange is high, and a common goal is shared. This is a type of team in which many people have taken part: it is a task force (also called a project team). Task forces are formed to address a specific issue, and they know that once they complete their task their job is over. Getting task forces up and running calls for a specific type of team building.

Task forces work on unstructured tasks. The ultimate goal may be clear, but the best route to take to get there is not. Task forces are problem solvers. Therefore, the primary concern for task forces is to hammer out a plan of action to work toward that goal. There are various ways to do this, which will be discussed later; at this point, suffice it to say that clearly articulating the short-term goals that will facilitate moving toward the longer-term aim is imperative for task forces.

Most of the time, the roles of task force members are ill-defined. Thus, they need to think about how to allocate the various short-term goals and their roles so that the ultimate goal can be reached. It is easy at this point in the life of a task force to get bogged down in the nuts and bolts of who is going to do what and when. If a task force gets bogged down so that team members are not using their time constructively, then an intervention to deal directly with the who-does-what-and-when is an especially fruitful approach to enhancing the work of the task force. Because each member needs to carve out an individual role—preferably with the consent of the rest of the task force—replacing task force members is something to avoid if possible. Each member has a unique role to play and all members of the task force know the role of each one, but those roles are not readily apparent to an outsider.

One of the curious characteristics of task forces is their political makeup. Often members of a task force are not brought into the group because of their skills or expertise, but instead to represent the views of a particular constituency. Whether this is the case—and to what degree—is critical to determining whether the task force can complete its work. The roles of political members must be clearly understood by all of the other members.

The roles of task force members should fit their individual skills and interests. It is very important to divide up the work in a manner such that either the strengths of each member are played up or the tasks are of inherent interest to each member; with a good division of tasks, even a relatively unskilled team member will be highly motivated to contribute. Here again, interventions in task forces can examine the way the work has been divided to ascertain if there are opportunities for improvement.

Communication links between members of a task force are many, and all members have a chance to voice their opinions. It has to be so, because everyone on the task force must have a sense of ownership of the final product. Task forces should have frequent meetings to discuss and clarify their goals, their individual roles, how work is progressing on the various fronts, what stumbling blocks the members have run across, and so on. Efficient meetings are a must for task forces; otherwise, it is easy for them to get sidetracked onto irrelevant issues.

Task forces usually are not "led," but instead are "chaired." The distinction here is critical. The chair of a task force often has no more formal authority than the other members of the group. The chair's special functions include being the liaison between the task force and other groups, calling meetings, and ensuring that the task force continually moves toward its goal. Decisions are consensual. When conflicts arise that threaten movement toward the goal, some sort of decision-making strategy needs to be invoked. If a strategy has not been decided on, then the task force may easily be stalled.

Information exchange between task force members is also determined at the initial meetings of the task force: timing of what gets delivered, to whom, and where. The more these expectations are specified, the fewer the problems task forces encounter in completing their work on time and within budget.

As already noted, task forces usually share a long-term goal. This is helpful because it keeps the task force "on track" at the macro level. However, the phrase "The devil is in the details" is quite apt in describing task forces. The detailing of all the short-term goals, subtasks, and member roles must be negotiated. A set of mechanisms for accomplishing this work is necessary.

This description should make it apparent that a task force approach to team building is appropriate when there is a specific problem to solve that is complex enough to need the knowledge, skills, and abilities of more than one or two individuals. Task forces work best when the ultimate outcome is clearly delineated and the schedule is limited. Task force members know that when the job is completed they will no longer be working together.

Clearly, not all work lends itself to a task force approach. If the work drags on, members become frustrated and discouraged. Task forces need a lot of "up front" help defining outcomes of their work before they get started. The more fully this preparation is done, the better able the task force will be to function down the road.

Standing or Functional Teams: Teams with a Long-Term Goal

For the final "pure" example of a team, think about the following working conditions: tasks are multiple and dynamic, the team members' roles are undifferentiated, communication is used as needed, need for information exchange is moderate and continual, and both goals and stakeholders are many. Teams that operate under these conditions are called standing or functional teams. This is the most common type of work group in organizations today. A collection of individuals comes together for an indefinite period of time to work on several different tasks. In standing teams, the knowledge of each member's characteristics is very important. More than in any other type of work group, standing team members need to be able to work together for the long term. Even if they do not like one another, they have to respect one another's strengths and know one another's weaknesses. Over the years at a place of employment standing team members get to know one another very well.

Because the tasks that standing teams work on are numerous, interventions can be useful to prioritize work and determine what can actually get accomplished so that the team feels it is successful. Standing teams often do not receive the type and amount of feedback that crews and task forces receive. Thus, feedback mechanisms for these teams must be built if they don't exist. I am constantly surprised at how many teams in organizations have no way to gauge their successes.

Standing team members may very well have overlapping skills. The membership on the team is often by default; that is, the team is made up of individuals who used to constitute a department or unit. These individuals now are expected to act like members of a team.

It takes more time and effort to get standing teams to think and act like a team than to get crews or task forces to do so. Because the standing team's tasks are so many, so varied, and all a high priority, it is easy for individual team members to go off and work by themselves and convince themselves that they are accomplishing something. Although they may indeed be working on appropriate tasks, it may also be the case that they are not. Thus, finding, articulating, and adhering to a set of common goals is essential to getting standing teams to operate effectively.

Standing team members need to know how their roles are feeding into the team's goals. They need to have the organization's goals spelled out clearly so that they can ensure the team's goals are aligned properly. They need to know how they fit into the organization as a team.

Communication between members of a standing team is ad hoc and usually occurs when there is a problem to be worked out. Often there is no designated leader or chair who performs the liaison role for the team, even though standing teams need someone in this role just as much as do crews and task forces.

Information exchange between members is also often ad hoc and based on working on a particular task that may or may not involve the entire team. One characteristic of standing teams is that although they are nominally a team, they often function independently on a day-to-day basis. It is possible for standing teams not to meet for months at a time. If this is the case, then when they do meet it is important for team members to catch up with one another.

Because of the high degree of discretion standing team members have over how they spend their time in a workday, it becomes even more important that the team's overarching goals be kept in mind. The goals provide a source of stability for the team members and a sense of oneness that might otherwise be missing.

Standing teams require a lot of time on the organization's part and on the team members' part to get up and running. It may be several months before the members of a standing team actually feel as though they are part of a team. Team performance management systems as well as reward and recognition systems are very important. If the organization is not willing to commit time and effort to the "teaming" process, then the standing team members will quickly revert back to their individual status and not act like members of a group.

Assessing Team Type

Figure 2.1 represents crews, task forces, and standing teams as examples of the more general concept of team. Although pure forms of each of these team types

FIGURE 2.1. TEAM TYPES.

are easy to visualize, it is also pertinent to note that teams may take on characteristics of all three types or may move from one type to another over time. For example, a standing team may divide into smaller task force units. Or sometimes task forces are together for so long that they really are, in effect, standing teams. And some crews have more discretion over their tasks than other crews, and so may feel more like standing teams.

The statements presented in Exhibit 2.2 are useful as points of departure for discussion to help team members determine what type of team they form. Through this kind of discussion, they may think through what will be the most effective interventions for their team.

Issues for Different Team Types

Because teams can take on the characteristics of different types at different points in their history or when different tasks come their way, it is relevant to ask the question, "Does it matter what type of team this is?" The answer is yes. McGrath, Berdahl, and Arrow (1995) are quite clear in their recommendation that different types of teams benefit from different approaches to enhancing their work. For crews, ensure that tasks are very structured and the mechanisms for communication and work flow between members are clearly understood and consistently utilized. For task forces, define the goals to accomplish the task and define the roles of the members. For standing teams, prioritize work tasks and get people to work together as a team.

In other words, crews, task forces, and standing teams all work in different contexts. For each different type of team, particular attention must be paid to certain issues more than to other issues. The following chapters present a number of places in which to intervene to make teams successful. Which specific interventions will provide the most effective levers for enhancing team performance will depend on the type of team.

EXHIBIT 2.2. MEASURING TEAM TYPE.

These questions can stimulate a great deal of discussion among team members. As an exercise, have the team members complete the items on their own, and then bring the team together to see how closely individuals' perceptions of the team match the perceptions of others. If the team members agree on these items, the team is more likely to function well than if they do not agree.

Read each item and determine the extent to which you agree with it. Interpretation of the scores is provided after the items.

	Completely disagree	Disagree somewhat	Neither agree nor disagree	Agree somewhat	Completely agree
Crew Items					
1. Members of my team have specialized, highly trained, noninterchangeable skill sets.	1	2	3	4	5
2. Members of my team have specialized roles.	1	2	3	4	5
3. The roles of my team members were set before the team ever met.	1	2	3	4	5
4. A member of my team can easily be replaced with another individual with a similar set of skills.	1	2	3	4	5
5. Members of my team communicate with a distinct line of authority.	1	2	3	4	5
6. Members of my team complete their work within a hierarchical model.	1	2	3	4	5
7. The outcomes of my team are known and shared collectively by all team members.	1	2	3	4	5
8. The work processes that move my team toward its ultimate goal(s) are known and shared collectively by all team members.	1	2	3	4	5

	Completely disagree	Disagree somewhat	Neither agree nor disagree	Agree somewhat	Completely agree
Task Force Items					
1. My team knows it has a fixed period of time to accomplish its work.	1	2	3	4	5
2. The end goal(s) of my team are well-defined, but the process by which to accomplish the goal(s) is ill-defined.	1	2	3	4	5
3. My team had to set up a communication system.	1	2	3	4	5
4. My team had to set up a system to resolve conflicts.	1	2	3	4	5
5. Some team members were selected to be part of the team to serve political rather than functional ends.	1	2	3	4	5
6. The roles of each team member needed to be defined.	1	2	3	4	5
7. It is difficult to replace members of my team because of the knowledge/history each member carries.	1	2	3	4	5
8. The chairship of my team was an issue that needed to be resolved, in terms of both who had the role and what its function was.	1	2	3	4	5
Standing Team Items					
1. My team is together for an indefinite period of time.	1	2	3	4	5
2. Team members have multiple, often independent goals.	1	2	3	4	5
3. It is difficult to prioritize the work that my team as a whole is supposed to accomplish.	1	2	3	4	5

EXHIBIT 2.2. (*continued*)

	Completely disagree	Disagree somewhat	Neither agree nor disagree	Agree somewhat	Completely agree
4. My team has multiple stakeholders.	1	2	3	4	5
5. Members of my team serve in multiple roles on the team.	1	2	3	4	5
6. Change in the composition of team membership is bound to occur.	1	2	3	4	5
7. Members of my team also serve another function in a different part of the organization.	1	2	3	4	5
8. Feedback to my team is sparse and/or sporadic.	1	2	3	4	5

Note: Add up the scores for each of the three sets of crew, task force, and standing team items separately. Scores can range from 8 to 40. A score below 16 on any team dimension is considered low. Scores between 16 and 31 are considered midrange. A score above 32 is considered high.

The ratings on each of the dimensions should provide the team members with a sense of what type of team they believe they are. For example, a team may have rated itself "high" on being a crew, "midrange" on being a task force, and "low" on being a standing team.

CHAPTER THREE

RESOURCES TEAMS NEED

One of the most frustrating problems in any kind of work is having insufficient resources. This frustration is multiplied when team members work together. A model often cited in the team performance research literature is one by Hackman (1987). He proposed that the material resources provided to the team would affect the relationship between how the work got done by the team and the outcomes the team produced. That is, the more resources the team had, the more likely it was that the work processes would lead to successful work outcomes. Conversely, the fewer resources the team had, the less likely it was that the work processes would lead to successful work outcomes.

In my work I have found that resources come into play much earlier in the team performance model. That is, if the team does not have the resources up front, the team will not get started appropriately and the delay will have negative ramifications as the team progresses to carry out its work.

In this chapter, I'll describe each of the resources in turn as they relate to team performance. Next, as points of departure and discussion for teams to use as they begin to define their own resource needs, I will provide examples of ways to determine resource needs. This chapter will be of special interest to those working on teams for which resources are an issue.

Resource Categories

The resources teams need can be categorized in the same way as other organizational resources: physical, financial, and human. In addition, a resource that seems to be more and more scarce these days—as organizations have downsized and are trying to do more with less—is personnel time. This is distinct from human resources in general. Traditionally, personnel time might have been perceived as part of human resources, yet human resources are usually accounted for in terms of number of bodies. It is more important to see exactly how those bodies are spending their time—and in particular, from a team perspective, how much time the team members are engaged in team activity versus individual activity. Just about anyone who works for an organization full-time seems to be too busy. As a result, the resources that teams need most as they are trying to get up and running—people's time and commitment—are in short supply.

Physical Resources

Accounting personnel are familiar with physical resources and usually refer to them as *assets for the organization*. These are capital budget line items that depreciate or appreciate over time. Physical resources available to a team include items such as computer hardware, computer software, physical space, storage room, and anything else that can be seen or touched.

Despite the importance of physical resources to the functioning of most organizations, teams often either overlook the physical resources that they have or fail to identify those that they need. Yet teams need to think about the physical resources they must have to operate effectively. For most teams, physical resources are simply a given. They are provided to the team or simply come to the team because they belonged to a team member when that member was assigned to be part of the team.

Financial Resources

Financial resources are cash or other resources that can readily be turned into cash. This cash can be used by the team to buy goods and services needed to complete its work. Any team that works within an operating budget is very familiar with its financial resources. Most teams, however, do not have any liquid finances to manage. This state of affairs is counterproductive. If a team is accountable for its spending practices, it is more likely to perceive itself as a team.

Think of it in the following manner: One child receives an allowance to spend as she will. The other child asks her parent or guardian for the things she wants as she wants them. Who will learn more quickly about the value of what money can and can't purchase? Similarly, imagine a team that is asked to carry out a task. If the team is given a budget with which to do it and if any part of the task not completed within budget will be completed on the team members' own time or with their own money, then the team will have to become aware of the cost of doing business.

Human Resources

Human resources are the personnel available to the team to complete its work. Sometimes individual members work on the team full-time; often the team is just another part of these individuals' jobs and each person devotes only a certain number of hours to the team. Some individuals are members of several teams within the same organization. Therefore, it is important that each team member is on the team for a particular reason.

An individual may be on the team to provide specific *knowledge*. This knowledge may be technical (for example, how to run a particular software package, what stress level a particular road bed can handle, how to analyze a data set) or people-oriented (for example, knowing to whom to talk to get a job done, being familiar with a particular client, representing a particular advocacy group's concerns).

A person may be on the team to provide specific *skills*. These skills can take many forms as well, ranging from oral presentation and written communication skills, to expertise in organizing, facilitating groups, handling irate customers, closing a sale, or woodworking.

Finally, an individual may be on the team because of specific *abilities*. These abilities may include anything from creative thinking, to being able to work long hours for a lengthy period of time, to being upbeat in the presence of negative information.

One of the most common questions about teams is, "How large should the team be?" The answer is, "However many it takes to do the job and no more." In other words, there is no optimal number. Large teams can distribute work so that each member carries less, but large teams are also difficult to coordinate. Small teams can be very easy to manage, but members may easily become overworked or may lack specific skills to do the job. So before answering the question of "How many people?" the first questions to answer are "What is the task?" and "How many people do we need to accomplish the task?"

Personnel Time Resources

Although somewhat tied to human resources, over the past decade personnel time has taken on a life of its own. That is, employees have certain amounts of time to devote to any one thing, and they are having to prioritize their work in ways that make best use of their time available. In the mid-1990s team members began to comment about their time when they were asked about the physical, financial, and human resources available to them. The comments centered on the perception that they did not have adequate time to get up and running as a team, complete the tasks at a high-quality level, interact with clients, interact with their supervisors, or interact with one another to pass along relevant information. Since then, I have been asking teams to rate the extent to which they feel they are provided enough time to complete their work in an effective manner. Almost all of them rate this item as "not enough."

The issue of adequate time requires some thought—particularly for teams that are just starting out or are making modifications in their structure or processes. There is a learning curve associated with determining the amount of time needed to complete work. If teams are not allowed the time to organize themselves properly, then they are less likely to succeed. Adequate time for completing tasks and exchanging information needs to be built into the process of teamwork. All too often, time is not taken into account when determining how well a team has performed. It is a mistake to discount the degree to which time has had an impact on the team's performance.

Planning for Resource Needs

What is proposed here is that the team should take a systematic look at what physical, financial, human, and time resources it has to work with; document them; and determine what other resources, if any, need to be procured now and in the future. To make this determination, the team needs to set out its tasks over a defined period of time. For example, if a team at a retail clothing store is expected to develop a new system for handling customer complaints, then the tasks associated with that goal must be logically and concretely laid out, and the physical, financial, human, and time resources that are needed must be understood by all parties.

Project teams will be familiar with this type of work, as project teams often must create a proposal to bid on particular jobs. Most bids have a price tag attached to the proposal, so that someone has actually had to do the cost accounting for the project. For many teams, however, this type of activity is unfamiliar territory. Luckily there is nothing mysterious about the process.

The best way to become familiar with this aspect of team functioning is to work through several examples. Three examples are provided here for teams to examine, think about, and learn from (see Exhibits 3.1, 3.2, and 3.3). Listed are all the tasks and all possible resources that might be needed in each example. They are very detailed. Although some of the resources may not actually be needed, it is helpful to determine all possible needs before embarking on a task.

I have provided three examples because in my experience, being able to make accurate resource determinations is difficult and takes a lot of practice. Teams that require less practice can skip over the examples. Those that need more practice can use the examples to their benefit. In addition, whether one, two, or all three examples are studied, teams need to go through the same type of exercise using tasks that are relevant in their own work situations.

Benefits of Resource Needs Planning

The benefit to your team of engaging in this seemingly tedious resource planning process will become apparent soon after doing the exercise; here is how it can work. After the team has used the resource planning process for a couple of months, the team members assess the adequacy of the resources allocated to them to accomplish their work using the items in Exhibit 3.4.

If the team rates the adequacy of the resources as insufficient, there should be a way to make a case for investing more resources in the team or otherwise for scaling back expectations of the team. To do this, the team must make a case in a rational, logical, and documented manner.

Assuming that the team has done its resource needs planning appropriately and each team member has acted in good faith to carry his or her share of the workload, then if the team is experiencing resource problems it will have a strong case to make with the supervisor or organization about securing the needed resources in the future. Thus, this preparation will help the team by ensuring that necessary resources are available. This is the first step in the Team Performance Model. With adequate resources, the team is on its way to effective performance.

EXHIBIT 3.1. RESOURCE NEEDS PLANNING: EXAMPLE ONE.

The issue: Write a manual for Web page policy. Assume you are a five-person standing team in the information systems department in an organization.

Tasks	Physical Resources[a]	Financial Resources[b]	Human Resources[c]	Time[d]
a. Determine end users of the manual.	Meeting room for team members; Access to e-mail system to contact end users; Database system to collect information about end users; Database collating system to organize information about end users (i.e., who would use what information)		Knowledge of who all potential end users are	Meeting (10 hours); End user determination (15 hours)
b. Examine other manuals of the organization for consistency of presentation.	Access to other manuals in the organization; Access to word processing package for similar presentation style	Cost of securing other manuals	Ability to procure manuals from other areas in the organization	Compiling other manual prototypes (4 hours)
c. Examine Web page policy manuals from other organizations.	Access to Web browsers to identify and contact Web masters at different organizations; Access to other organizations' manuals	Cost of securing other organizations' manuals	Knowledge of other organizations that might have Web policy manuals; Knowledge of how to get other Web policy manuals	Examining other Web policy manuals and compiling the information (8 hours)
d. Outline the contents of the manual.	Meeting room for team members; Access to word processor; Access to photocopier		Skill in organizing written information; Previous experience writing manuals	Meeting (10 hours)
e. Submit outline to end users for feedback.	Access to e-mail or other address information of end users; Database system to collect information from end users; Database collating system to organize the information from end users (comments on the outline)	Remuneration to end users for their time	Knowledge of different types of potential end users; Interpersonal skills in getting assistance from end users; Contacts at higher levels in the organization to communicate organizational endorsement of the task publicly	Contacting and compiling of information from end users, assuming five end users sampled (10 hours)
f. Assign sections to team member(s) to collect information.	Meeting room to meet team members		Ability to determine length of sections and how much work might be involved in each one; Skills specifically needed in each section, allocated to appropriate individual	Meeting (5 hours)

Task	Physical resources	Financial resources	Skills	Time estimate
g. Team members collect information.	Computers available to each member to collect information and organize it Word processing packages similar across team members to facilitate collation		Skill in determining where to find relevant information. Word processing skills	Collecting and collating information gathered (25 hours)
h. Assign collation of draft 1 to a team member.	Meeting room for team members		Writing skills	Collating draft 1 (5 hours)
i. Review draft 1 manual.	E-mail or other contact address for the team member who collated draft 1 for return comments		Editing skills	Reviewing draft 1 and providing feedback (5 hours)
j. Make modifications to draft 1.	Computer available Word processing available Photocopier available		Writing skills	Revising draft 1 (5 hours)
k. Send draft 2 to subset of end users.	E-mail or other contact address for subset of end users E-mail or other contact address for the team member who collated draft 2 for return comments	Remuneration to end users for their time	Knowledge of potential end users who would be willing to spend time examining the draft carefully Interpersonal skills in getting assistance from end users	Contacting end users, reviewing draft 2, obtaining end user feedback, assuming five end users sampled (15 hours)
l. Revise draft 2 into final manual.	Computer available		Writing skills	Revising draft 2 into final policy manual (5 hours)
m. Make sufficient number of copies of manual.	Printing facilities available	Printing costs	Administrative skills Knowledge of the organization's printing facilities	Copying/printing (1 hour)
n. Distribute manual.	Distribution facility available	Distribution costs	Administrative skills Knowledge of the organization's distribution facilities	Distributing (1 hour)

[a] Some assumptions regarding the usual availability of physical resources can be made, given that the information systems team is part of the organization. For example, a meeting room could presumably be booked at the organization. Similarly, e-mail, e-mail, faxes, printing, and distribution facilities are commonly available to teams in an organization. It is useful, however, to note what the team will need. Then if there is a physical resource unique to the task, the team will have had the foresight to secure it before it is needed.

[b] Several of the items associated with this task have no direct financial costs, given the context of the issue. The information systems team is part of the organization, so presumably the team will not have to purchase all goods and services. In addition, remuneration for end users' time may not be necessary in an organization; however, some organizations do account for employee time very strictly and even enforce interdepartmental billing, so the example includes this remuneration as a financial cost.

[c] Notice that the human resources are listed not in terms of people but in terms of knowledge, skills, and abilities. Although hypothetical, this exercise does provide a flavor for how to go about staffing a team. It may be that there is a large standing team in the information systems department, a subset of which has been charged with this particular task. Whom to put on the task should be determined by the characteristics needed in the human resources planning exercise.

[d] The time estimates are based on a number of assumptions. When teams actually go through this exercise with tasks of their own with which they are familiar, it is enlightening for the members to think through carefully how and where time is being spent. In this example it is not just the information systems team's time that needs to be accounted for, but the end users' time as well. This time is a cost to the organization, because if the end users are helping with the Web policy manual they are not doing something else.

EXHIBIT 3.2. RESOURCE NEEDS PLANNING: EXAMPLE TWO.

The issue: Carry out an evaluation of client service satisfaction. Assume you are a task force made up of five sales supervisors in a retail department store.

Tasks	Physical Resources	Financial Resources	Human Resources	Time[a]
a. Determine who the clients are (e.g., suppliers, customers).	Meeting room Flip chart Computer to record information Word processing package to record information	Consultant or facilitator costs	Knowledge of all different clients	Meeting to determine who the clients are (10 hours)
b. Determine what is meant by satisfaction (e.g., satisfaction with what?).	Meeting room Flip chart Computer to record information Word processing package to record information	Consultant or facilitator costs	Knowledge of various clients' different areas of possible satisfaction or dissatisfaction	Meeting to determine what is meant by satisfaction (10 hours)
c. Determine the best way to collect information on client satisfaction (e.g., interview, survey, questionnaire).	Meeting room Flip chart Computer to record information Word processing package to record information	Consultant costs	Skills in determining the best method to get at the question that is needing to be answered Knowledge of how much time, energy, and cost are associated with the different possible ways to collect the data	Meeting to determine the best way to collect information (10 hours)
d. Determine how many customers to get information from.	Meeting room Flip chart Computer to record information Word processing package to record information	Consultant costs	Knowledge of the number in the targeted client group Knowledge of sampling and confidence in results based on sample sizes	Meeting to determine how many customers to get information from (5 hours)
e. Determine the length of time for data collection.	Meeting room Flip chart Computer to record information Word processing package to record information Word processing package to record information	Consultant costs	Knowledge of how frequently clients are engaged with organizational personnel Knowledge of how many clients are likely to be in contact with the organization over a given time period Knowledge of how best to solicit participation from clients	Meeting to determine the length of time for data collection (5 hours)

Task	Facilities/Equipment/Materials	Nonpersonnel Costs	Knowledge and Skills	Personnel Time (Hours)
f. Design the data collection device (e.g., interview, survey, question-naire).		Consultant costs	Knowledge and skill in survey/questionnaire/interview design	Designing the data collection device (30 hours)
g. Collect the data.	Telephones if telephone survey used / Photocopy/printing of questionnaires or surveys / Writing instruments	Photocopying/any long distance phone call-ing/mailing costs	Contact clients / Time to spend collecting information / Interpersonal skills / Listening skills / Questioning skills	Collecting the data (10 hours)
h. Enter data into database.	Computer for data storage / Database management package to store information	Hardware and software costs	Data entry skills / Typing skills	Entering data into database (20 hours)
i. Analyze data.	Computer for data analysis / Data analysis software package	Hardware and software costs	Data analysis skills	Analyzing data (30 hours)
j. Write a report on the findings.	Computer for report writing / Word processing package for report writing / Photocopier to make multiple copies of the report	Printing costs	Writing skills / Skill in organizing written information	Writing report on the findings (30 hours)
k. Make oral presentation of the findings to management.	Meeting room / Computer for presentation / Screen for presentation / Photocopies of slides/overheads	Copying costs	Oral presentation skills / Skill in using presentation technology	Orally presenting the findings to management (20 hours)

a Again, the situation here is hypothetical. In estimating hours, an assumption was that the five-member task force would collect data from about six to ten clients. Therefore, no training of sales personnel was needed. If this were a larger-scale project, then perhaps sales personnel would also be expected to collect the data and have to be trained in how to do so. Such an approach would add line items to each of the resource areas listed.

EXHIBIT 3.3. RESOURCE NEEDS PLANNING: EXAMPLE THREE.

The issue: Decide whether to expand the business into a new service line, and if so, when. Assume you are the top management team (made up of five partners) in an automotive sales industry. The following tasks associated with this issue could be carried out by the team members themselves, by other members of the organization, or by external consultants. In making the estimates, it is assumed that the five-member team will be doing the work.

Tasks	Physical Resources	Financial Resources	Human Resources	Time
a. Examine the financial viability of all existing service lines.	Access to information on all service lines—including, but not limited to, accounting books, audited information, customer service flow, any other documentation on existing service lines	Data collection costs (which may include an outside consultant)	Knowledge of the service lines Financial expertise to review all parts of the business	Collecting and organizing information (200 hours)
b. Study the existing service providers in the line into which the automotive sales group is thinking of expanding to determine how financially viable the existing service providers are and how they conduct their businesses.	Access to any public information regarding existing service providers Access to any private information regarding existing service providers to gather the same type of data	Data collection costs (which may include an outside consultant)	Knowledge of existing service providers Financial expertise to review potential competitor businesses Personal contacts of the top management team	Collecting and organizing information (200 hours)
c. Analyze the market to determine if it will handle another service provider.	Access to market information (demographic characteristics of potential customers, customer needs, etc.)	Data collection costs (which may include an outside consultant)	Knowledge and skill in carrying out a market analysis	Collecting and organizing information (200 hours)
d. Determine costs of expanding service in terms of physical location.	Information on potentially desirable locations Information on size of location needed Information on lease and zoning arrangements Information on costs for space	Data collection costs (which may include an outside consultant)	Knowledge of physical locations Knowledge and skill in leasing and zoning arrangements	Collecting and organizing information (100 hours)

Task	Information/Resources	Costs	Knowledge/Skills	Time
e. Determine costs of expanding service in terms of financial expenditures needed up front.	Information on how financing can be handled Information on the amount of financing needed	Data collection costs (which may include an outside consultant)	Knowledge of financial options available Knowledge and skill in negotiating financial agreements	Collecting and organizing information (100 hours)
f. Determine human resource needs for staffing and operating new service line.	Identification of the knowledge, skills, and abilities needed of staff Information on how many staff members would be needed	Data collection costs (which may include an outside consultant)	Assessment of the knowledge, skills, and abilities that will be necessary for the new service line Knowledge of the present human resource market in terms of personnel availability and costs to secure the personnel	Collecting and organizing information (100 hours)
g. Determine the most appropriate timing for opening the new service line.	Information on any economic cycles that will have an impact on the potential market	Data collection costs (which may include an outside consultant)	Knowledge of any economic cycles in the marketplace	Collecting and organizing information (50 hours)
h. Determine how the new service line would fit into the existing organizational structure.	Information on the present organizational structure Information on current operational processes	Data collection costs (which may include an outside consultant)	Knowledge of the present organizational structure Knowledge of the present organizational processes	Collecting and organizing information (200 hours)
i. Determine what members of the team would oversee what aspects of the new service line.	Meeting room for team members	Consultant or facilitator costs	Skill in integrating new aspects of a business into an existing business Skill in determining team members' strengths and interest in the new service line	Meeting to discuss new line (40 hours)
j. Determine whether to proceed.	Meeting room for team members	Consultant or facilitator costs	Skill in facilitating a group decision-making process	Meeting to determine whether to proceed, including the time needed by members to review all material collected to this point (200 hours)

EXHIBIT 3.4. RESOURCE ASSESSMENT.

First, each team member reads the items and determines the extent to which he or she agrees with the statement. Next, meet as a team and discuss the agreement ratings selected by each individual team member. Then come to an agreement and provide a single "team" rating. Finally, invite the team manager to attend a meeting at which these issues can be discussed. It is most effective for the team to speak to the manager with one voice after considering the issues one at a time.

	Completely disagree	Disagree somewhat	Neither agree nor disagree	Agree somewhat	Completely agree
1. The physical resources provided to my team to complete its work are adequate.	1	2	3	4	5
2. The financial resources provided to my team to complete its work are adequate.	1	2	3	4	5
3. The human resources provided to my team to complete its work are adequate.	1	2	3	4	5
4. The time provided to my team to complete its work is adequate.	1	2	3	4	5

CHAPTER FOUR

THE CONTEXT OF TEAMWORK

The environment in which teams work on a day-to-day basis has a substantial impact on their ability to perform. The research evidence is quite clear in this regard (for example, Kline & MacLeod, 1997; Shea & Guzzo, 1987a). Thus, the organization needs to spend some time and effort reviewing the policies, procedures, and overall environment to examine the degree to which the context fosters teamwork. Although this is a time-consuming task and most organizations will be reluctant to take the time to do it, it is well worth the effort.

Considering the Overall Context

A number of general contextual areas need to be scrutinized. Exhibit 4.1 is a quick organizational assessment tool that introduces these areas. Team members should complete all the items as a unit. Discussion about these items will provide the team with some sense of where and how much the organizational context actually supports teamwork. Using those results, teams can alert the organization about those areas where more support is needed. In addition, where the organization is supportive of teams, members should be quick to indicate that they appreciate that support and that the support contributes to their overall performance.

EXHIBIT 4.1. MEASURING ORGANIZATIONAL SUPPORT.

First, each team member reads the items and determines the extent to which he or she agrees with the statement. Next, meet as a team and discuss the agreement ratings selected by each individual team member. Then come to an agreement and provide a single "team" rating, or alternatively average across team members to reach an aggregate score. Interpretation of the scores is provided after the items.

	Completely disagree	Disagree somewhat	Neither agree nor disagree	Agree somewhat	Completely agree
1. Teams are formally espoused in this organization.	1	2	3	4	5
2. The reward system is set up to recognize team performance.	1	2	3	4	5
3. Support systems for teams are well established.	1	2	3	4	5
4. Teams are readily differentiated in the organization.	1	2	3	4	5
5. Teams are well integrated into the organization's line functions.	1	2	3	4	5
6. The organization's goals are well articulated.	1	2	3	4	5
7. Team goals are aligned with those of the organization.	1	2	3	4	5

Note: Add up the scores for each of the items. Scores can range from 7 to 35. A score below 15 indicates that the organizational context is not very supportive of teamwork. Scores between 15 and 27 indicate that the organizational context is somewhat supportive of teamwork. A score above 28 indicates that the organizational context is highly supportive of teamwork.

Each of the seven specific items will be discussed in turn in the following paragraphs. In addition to providing diagnostic information about the organizational context, these items offer ideas about where the organization can improve in supporting teams.

Espousal of Teamwork

This measure gets at the extent to which teams and the team approach to work are actually part of the organization's work structure and work processes. This kind of formalization can be demonstrated in various ways, including incorporating the importance of teams into manuals on policies and procedures, annual reports, speeches given by upper management, and mission or vision statements. Another way is to show teams as the identifiable work units on the organizational chart. Other ways to formalize the importance of teams are to recognize the "team player of the month," to advertise for and select employees who fit well into a team environment, and to design the office layout so that teams are geographically located together.

Schein (1990) refers to formalization efforts of this type as *artifacts* of the organization's culture. These artifacts are part of a broader category that includes office design, dress code, products, and the like. They are what one feels or observes as one enters the premises. Schein notes that artifacts are sometimes hard to interpret. When it comes to teams, for example, the artifacts may not indicate how meaningful teams are to the day-to-day functioning of the organization. The types of formalization noted provide a signal, at least on the surface, that the organization believes that teams are important. Whether organizations then "put their money where their mouth is" on the team issue is another matter—which is addressed by the remaining questions.

Reward System

One of the more eye-opening discoveries I made when I began to work with teams was the lack of formal team evaluation systems in organizations that proclaimed themselves to be team-based. Specifically, when I began my research in this field, I needed to have some way to evaluate how effective teams were at their jobs. The best place to find out this information, I thought, would be to ask teams directly how they were evaluated. Surprisingly, *none* of the twenty-odd teams I interviewed had any evaluation associated with their work *as a team*. This is not to say that the individual members were not evaluated—they were. The members were evaluated as individual workers. Thus began a study that was designed solely to examine how best to evaluate teams. The methods we used for this study (Kline

& McGrath, 1998) and the work that details what we found is discussed fully in Chapter Nine, "Evaluating Team Outcomes."

What became clear from this work is that teams want to be—and need to be—evaluated as a unit. Although not all team members wanted to have all of their compensation tied directly to how well the team performed, most expressed a keen interest in having at least part of their compensation tied to their team's performance. This issue is important in terms of making the team perceive itself as a functioning, viable unit.

Implementing such a performance management system is complex. Individual salary structures are tied to pension plans, employee benefits, and the like. Leavitt (1975) suggests that this particular way to "take groups seriously" raises difficult and interesting problems for organizations. He notes that if nothing else, thinking about this issue will ensure that organizations begin to think creatively about pay and performance. If an organization decides to pursue the course of compensating workers at least partially on the basis of team performance, it signals very clearly and immediately to the team members that they are expected to operate as a team—rather than as individuals—and that, yes, indeed, the organization is taking teams seriously.

Support Systems

This measure gets at the notion that teams are not born; they must be made. At one end of the continuum are organizations that provide extensive training for teams. At the other end are organizations where teams have been foisted upon groups of employees with absolutely no assistance provided to them. More commonly, organizational support for teams lies somewhere in the middle.

What does this support look like? Basically, individual workers are often not aware of how to function like a team. Support can take the form of assistance at the beginning stages of team creation: to help members understand what type of team they are in, how they are expected to work together, what the team's strengths and weaknesses are, what the team's opportunities are, and what will threaten the team's performance. In addition, assistance in determining the performance expectations for the team is of great value in getting a team up and running.

Most teams are overwhelmed at the beginning stages of their development. Although Tuckman's forming, storming, norming, and performing stages (1965) have been shown to be of little or no assistance in getting teams to perform better, most teams do need to get a handle on what is expected of them; the earlier this understanding occurs, the faster the team can begin to work.

Once teams have set some initial goals and performance expectations, they have other support needs. First, it is helpful for most team members to learn how to call and run meetings effectively, as well as how many meetings to call and when. Second, if the team experiences problems with one or more of its individual members, support in how to deal with that challenge needs to be available. Third, resource procurement and allocation become more salient as team members actively begin to engage in their tasks.

This list of support needs is by no means complete. These are, however, some of the more important areas where teams seem to need help in functioning. As a result, the organization has a critical need for individuals who are specifically dedicated to helping teams work through their issues as they arise. These specialists need to be regularly available; teams usually don't anticipate their problems but instead come across them and may very well have trouble dealing with them. The more support available to the team, the more rapidly it can overcome any problems it encounters and get on with the business at hand.

Team Differentiation

Teams need to perceive themselves as somehow separate from the rest of the organization. The members should feel that they are part of an identifiable unit that performs as a unit. If team members do not have this feeling, then they do not constitute a team.

A number of concrete ideas about achieving this feeling of differentiation are being implemented in many organizations. One of the most important ways to get team members to be a team is to locate them geographically close together. This recommendation is not meant as an endorsement of open-office design; it is based instead on the idea that if team members run into one another more frequently, they are more likely to engage in conversations, solve problems, discuss issues, and the like. If teams are forced to call formal meetings to get members to come together from different buildings (or even different cities or countries), the informal chitchat is not going to happen. As a result, their interactions will always be formal, tightly controlled by time constraints, and infrequent.

Another way to get a team to feel distinctive is to name it, so that members can refer to themselves as belonging to Team Such-and-Such. In fact, the process of naming the team can be an enjoyable and interesting way to get team members talking about what is important to them about their tasks, what they want to have as outcomes, and other equally significant issues. It is not helpful to name it "Team 1" or "Team A." Such names are nondescriptive and do not engender a desire to be part of the entity. No CEO would call his or her company "Company X," and for very good reason. The same is true when it comes to naming a team.

If the team is to be in existence for an extended period of time, it might even be helpful to get the team its own logo or letterhead that can be used for external and internal communication. Coffee mugs, T-shirts, baseball caps, and other such paraphernalia are all indicators that the team is a unit unto itself. Memos from the senior management commenting on the team's work are another way to get the team to perceive itself as distinctive. Interactions by outsiders with the team as a whole, as opposed to with individual members, also make the team feel more distinctive.

These are only some suggestions of ways to get teams to function as distinctive units; there are many others.

Team Integration

Although integrating the team may at first glance appear to be the opposite of making it distinctive, it is not. The issue here is that the team's work must be viewed as vital to the success of the organization by its members, by individuals within the organization, and by outsiders. The more the team members believe that their contributions will enable them to perform well and thus enhance the organization's performance, the more likely they will be to put time and effort into their work.

The most salient example of how *not* to accomplish this integration is captured well by Lawler and Mohrman (1987) in their commentary on quality circles. They argue convincingly that one of the primary reasons for the failure of the quality circle movement in the 1980s was that, after a "honeymoon" period during which employees were solicited to spend time solving problems and providing input to the organization, disillusionment set in. During the honeymoon phase, employees were excited about being charged with the important task of making their organizations more effective. But the quality circles ran parallel to the line function of the organization as a whole; they had no way to implement their suggestions, no way to get around resistance to their suggestions. As a result, employees who had initially been highly motivated to take part in the quality circles resigned from them.

The lesson here is obvious. Although it is important for standing teams, it also is highly relevant to task forces, which are established to solve a particular problem or deal with a particular issue. If the members of these teams have no way to ensure that their hard work, time, and effort will pay off in some organizational change, they will refuse to participate on future teams. In contrast, if their work is valued, implemented, and recognized, the team members will likely want to work on another team. Furthermore, it is not only the team members who know about their work—*so do the other employees.* It may be very difficult to recruit new team members to work on a task if the employees know from watching their colleagues that all their time and effort will be for naught.

The closer the team's work is to the line or service function of the organization, the easier it is for team members to perceive their contributions as important. Sometimes it is necessary to articulate to the team exactly how it does fit into the organizational structure. This connection will be particularly relevant in organizations that restructure themselves, so that employees are not left trying to figure out what they really contribute to the organization in its reconfigured form.

Articulation of Organizational Goals

It is important that the team set goals for itself so that resource needs can be identified (see Chapter Three). Underlying this suggestion is the assumption that the organization has articulated its own goals and objectives; if it has done so then teams can use those organizational goals to guide their own goal-setting process.

Articulating goals is a greater problem than one might imagine. When speaking with teams about their performance, I invariably ask about the clarity of the organization's goals. In response, team members usually smile and shake their heads. So many organizations are reengineering, restructuring, engaging in strategic planning, and all other manner of activities falling under the rubric of change, that organizational goals for the next three years shift on a regular basis. This shifting is detrimental to team performance. Teams need some stability in what the organization values so that they can make decisions on a rational basis.

An organization that is serious about making its teams effective needs to clearly spell out its mission, what the organization cares about, and how teams' outputs will be evaluated against the criterion of the mission of the organization. Even better is for teams to have in hand the organization's business plan for the next three years. Members may be expected to become familiar with the plan and act accordingly.

Alignment of Team and Organizational Goals

It makes sense to talk about this issue only once the organization has articulated its own goals. For the sake of argument, it is assumed that the organization has indeed done its homework and that the teams within the organization understand fully where the organization is strategically headed.

It is here that the goals of the team are evaluated to determine how much sense they make in the big picture. The more closely the goals of the team are aligned with the organizational goals, the more successful the team is likely to be. If the team's goals are different from—or, worse, opposite to—those of the organization, then no degree of high-level performance by the team is going to be appreciated by the organization.

Reviewing each one of the team's goals and subgoals is the only way to make sure that alignment happens. It is easy sometimes to begin working on a task and then get sidetracked into an area that seems relevant at the time but leads the team into working on irrelevant tasks. Taking a step back once in a while during a team meeting is helpful; team members can review why they are doing what they are doing and how it all fits together.

Considering the Leader Context

The previous section dealt with the organizational context in a very broad sense. But one of the most critical contextual variables in making teams effective is the actions of the team leaders. Team leaders, as I use the term here, are *not* members of the team itself. The leaders are external to the team: the team reports to the leaders, and the leaders are ultimately responsible for the actions of the team. If this sounds like a supervisory role, in many ways it is. Depending on how much direction an individual team needs, leaders must change the way they interact with it; for highly autonomous teams the leader needs to adopt a more hands-off style, whereas if the team is dysfunctional the leader needs to adopt a more hands-on style until it is working smoothly again.

What kinds of actions should team leaders be expected to take? A lot has been written about managing work groups or managing teams and how the role of "controller" and "planner" has been replaced with that of "coach" or "facilitator" as organizations move toward a team-based workforce (for example, Jessup, 1990; Manz & Simms, 1989; Wellins, Byham, & Wilson, 1991). Despite the literature, a manageable list of what kinds of tasks team members expect their leaders to take on has not been readily available. So I decided to talk to team members and ask them myself.

Based on these discussions, the nine items contained in Exhibit 4.2 were developed to evaluate team leaders from the perspective of the team members. An examination of the items shows that items 1 to 5 evaluate the coach or facilitator role of the leader, whereas items 6 to 9 evaluate the leader's controller or planner role. When team members were asked, they generally wanted their leaders to be able to take on *both* the traditional controller or planner role and the new coach or facilitator role.

Although this preference may be bad news for team leaders in that they will have to do more than ever, it does not come as a surprise. Most teams are not autonomous and empowered. Most teams need some direction and help, particularly in clarifying what is expected of them. The individual best placed to do this is the leader.

EXHIBIT 4.2. MEASURING TEAM LEADERSHIP.

First, each team member reads the items and determines the extent to which he or she agrees with the statement. Next, meet as a team and discuss the agreement ratings selected by each individual team member. Then come to an agreement and provide a single team rating, or alternatively average across team members to reach an aggregate score. Meet with your team leader after your team has come to an agreement to discuss the results. Interpretation of the scores is provided after the items.

	Completely disagree	Disagree somewhat	Neither agree nor disagree	Agree somewhat	Completely agree
The Coach/Facilitator Role					
1. Our leader communicates a clear purpose for the team.	1	2	3	4	5
2. Our leader identifies available resources to assist our team.	1	2	3	4	5
3. Our leader acquires needed resources to assist our team.	1	2	3	4	5
4. Our leader develops team members' talents.	1	2	3	4	5
5. Our leader "runs interference" for our team.	1	2	3	4	5
The Controller/Planner Role					
6. Our leader deals effectively with team member conflict.	1	2	3	4	5
7. Our leader ensures that our team understands its constraints, resources, and problems.	1	2	3	4	5
8. Our leader plans and organizes tasks for our team.	1	2	3	4	5
9. Our leader coordinates our team's work activities.	1	2	3	4	5

Note: Adding up the scores for items 1 through 5 will give a total score for the coach/facilitator role of the team leader, with scores ranging from a low of 5 to a high of 25. A score of 10 or less indicates that the team leader is not a strong coach, a score between 11 and 19 indicates that the team leader performs reasonably well as a coach, a score of 20 or more indicates that the team leader is a good coach.

Adding up the scores for items 6 to 9 will give a total score for the controller/planner role of the team leader, with scores ranging from a low of 4 to a high of 20. A score of 8 or less indicates that the team leader is not a strong controller or planner, a score between 9 and 15

EXHIBIT 4.2. (*continued*)

indicates that the team leader performs reasonably well at controlling and planning, a score of 16 or more indicates that the team leader is a strong controller and planner.

The scores must be interpreted in light of the team's needs at the time. For example, a leader who scores high as a coach/facilitator and low as a controller/planner might be a poor combination for a team that is just starting out and needs help in the day-to-day running of its activities. Conversely, a leader who scores high as a controller/planner and low as a coach/facilitator might make for a smothering combination for a team that is used to a high degree of autonomy. Use the information you collect to have a meeting with your team leader. Discuss how the leader can better serve the needs of your team.

Like the first section of this chapter, this section will discuss in turn each of the nine items on the team leader effectiveness scale. In addition, some suggestions about how to improve team leadership will be provided.

Communicating a Clear Purpose

As indicated earlier, one of the most typical problems for a team is identifying clearly the issue on which it should spend its time and energy. Although the answer may be obvious for some teams (for example, a cockpit crew flying a 747), it often is not explicitly stated and the team has to go about clarifying the issue before beginning its work. Team leaders can be an invaluable source of assistance in accomplishing this task.

For example, leaders often are in a position to know more about the organization's direction than do team members. This big-picture knowledge can be of help in ensuring that the goals of the team are aligned with those of the organization. It can save the team valuable time and prevent having members "spin their wheels" on work that is not valued. Another example of how the leader can be of tremendous value is if the team is working on a problem that is politically sensitive. The leader can ensure that the team does not make a faux pas in the direction it takes or the methods it uses.

The leader can take the role of facilitator for team meetings that involve the identification and clarification of the team's purpose. He or she can and should assist the team whenever there is doubt about what the team is supposed to be doing.

Identifying Available Resources

There is a real need for team leaders to have access to administrative information to ensure that the task is carried out. Whether the resources are physical, financial, human, or time-based, the leader should be able to direct the team where to go to procure the resources it needs. In most organizations, direction of this kind means knowing the individuals who make the decisions about the resources. In bureaucratic organizations, it may also mean knowing what forms to fill out and where to get them. In other types of organizations, it may mean knowing the suppliers of various resources or, in the case of financial resources, the financial institutions that are likely to fund the team's work.

This part of the leader's role may make the leader sound more like an informational storehouse than anything else. Many team leaders might shrug this job off and say that the information is available if the team wants to go and find it. However, that approach is not helpful to most teams. Team members are far less likely than team leaders to have the necessary administrative connections within the organization, and they are less likely to know where to start to search for information. The leader is critical in ensuring that the team spends its time effectively going after the resources it needs.

The implication for team leaders is that they will need to spend a lot of time looking through manuals and other documentation in order to be facile in this particular role. It means they have to be familiar with other departments, with external agencies, and with suppliers. Thus, although this leader function is informational, it is also highly interactional, because the information is most often available through particular individuals who can facilitate any team's bid for resources.

Acquiring Needed Resources

Although this function is tied to the previous one, the types of leader activities associated with it are very different. Identifying resources is one thing; helping the team make a case and then supporting that case for actually procuring resources is quite another. This is very much an advocacy role for the leader. As advocate, the team leader needs to direct the team when it tries to make a case for itself for resource procurement.

The leader may help the team write a business plan to get external financial backing. The leader may help the team make a case for securing another individual to fulfill the personnel needs of the team. The team leader must know to whom the request is going to be directed so that the most effectively written or presented case is made. For example, a business plan needs to be highly detailed, and the audience may very well be external to the organization. In contrast, a request for additional personnel might be made orally to a busy senior administrator within the organization, so the leader will need to be brief and catchy when making the presentation.

Within the advocacy role there is a large informational component; that is, the leader needs to know who is going to receive the request and what is the best method to present it. In addition, both written and oral presentation skills are very important. The team might ask the leader to look over a draft of a written proposal or ask for help in writing the proposal from scratch. Team members might ask the leader to present the proposal to the powers that be or to watch and provide constructive feedback on a practice run of a presentation they are going to make. The team leader is expected to contribute to the team in all these ways.

Some teams require leaders to tackle more of these challenges than other teams. The level of expertise within the team itself will dictate how much of this type of activity the leader will need to engage in. However, team leaders should be aware that team members view this particular ability—helping them acquire resources—as a key one.

Developing Team Members' Talents

To play this role, the team leader is required to become familiar with each member's knowledge, skills, and abilities (KSAs). The leader will also need to know what KSAs the organization is likely to need in the future so that each team member can be counseled about what type of development activities he or she will need to continue to remain a productive team member. This is a career developer role.

It takes a lot of time for the team leader actually to carry out this role with each team member. The dividends, however, are very high. By knowing the skills that each member brings to the team, the leader has an overall view of the level of team skills available to do the team's work. This overview is critical for several reasons. From a selection standpoint, a new member should bring skills that add to the existing team skill set. From a training standpoint, training programs can be brought in as needed or team members can be sent to relevant training sessions to learn new skills that the team can use. From a development standpoint, team members appreciate (as do all employees, whether members of a team or not) that they have the opportunity to learn new skills in their work setting.

In fact, the opportunity to learn new skills is becoming a very important selling point for organizations trying to hire highly skilled individuals (for example, Cappelli and others, 1997; Kanter, 1989). Therefore, despite the difficulty of the time commitment, it is worth it in the long run if the leader is to execute this role properly. All in all, developing team members' talents makes teams more effective.

Running Interference

This is the protector role of the team leader. There are times when teams need to be buffered from requests and demands that are outside their mandate. There are times when teams are overburdened and cannot deal with more requests. There are times when teams are the target of criticism. These are the times when the leader needs to step between those who are external to the team and the team itself. The leader will need to be astute regarding the ramifications of protecting the team and will also have to be a good spokesperson so that the team is not perceived as blameworthy in situations where it is not to blame.

For example, if a patient dies while being operated on, the actions of all members of the operating team will likely be scrutinized to ensure that all that could be done was done—and this is as it should be. During the inquiry phase, the team members may feel very threatened and may be the target of negative attacks. The team leader, in this case probably the chief of surgery, needs to be aggressive in protecting the team members until the inquiry is completed. Otherwise, the team members will feel that they were left on their own, and even if the inquiry eventually finds all team members blameless they will have residual negative feelings toward their leader.

A less serious example is that of a team designated to evaluate the level of customer service provided by employees. Preliminary work finds that the scope of the job really is much larger than originally anticipated, but the team members perceive that the enlarged role is not part of the original agreement. The team leader needs to argue on their behalf that the project is much larger than was expected and therefore will require more time to complete. A team that is not protected by its leader from this type of role enlargement will not perform well because it will now be working on a different, larger task. Team members will also have very little respect for their leader if he or she does nothing on their behalf.

Dealing with Team Conflict

That team members wanted the leader to play this particular role came somewhat as a surprise. I had been expecting that self-directed, empowered team members would want to take care of intrateam conflict without interference by a supervisor. This was definitely *not* the case.

There are, of course, different types of conflict. There is a positive form of conflict where team members may disagree on a course of action, work through options in a systematic, collegial fashion, and come up with a solution that they can agree on. An example of how to do this will be discussed in Chapter Eight. Then there is the negative form of conflict, where a team member or members are disruptive and hinder the team from moving forward in its work. They are the team's naysayers, and they are difficult for most team members to work with. Problems can range from the member not carrying his or her weight to not supporting the team to others or just generally being negative about the task on which the team is working.

When the conflict is a positive one, the leader should not be involved unless asked to participate by the team members. Teams need to feel autonomous in their decision making, and the presence of the leader in decision-making contexts can have a negative impact on this sense of autonomy.

The opposite is true of negative conflict. Team members *want* the leader to intervene with negative members. In observing some teams where this was the case, it became clear that the other team members were ashamed of the negative individual but they were unable to act on the problem. It is very disruptive to a team if it must punish one of its own members. Many teams are made up of individuals at the same hierarchical level in the organization. There is usually no precedent or experience for them to draw on to show them how to reprimand a fellow employee. Therefore, members will be highly reluctant to chastise other members.

If the team is left on its own to cope with a negative individual, often the team will just suffer in silence. The other members will try to make up for the negative person by working around that person or even doing his or her work just so that they don't have to interact. This approach is detrimental to the team. It not only affects the work that the team can accomplish but also is very negative for the morale of the other team members.

So the leader is expected either to see that this situation exists or to respond to a request from the other team members and address the issue. The response may take the form of speaking to the negative member about the behavior and how it is expected to change, providing training for the member about how to be a more productive member of the team, or even threatening to remove the member from the team. Whatever the intervention, it needs to happen, and the sooner the better. Sometimes a negative member does not even realize the poor impact being made on the team. Other times the negative member will respond to nothing less than a threat of termination. Obviously, this role requires that the leader have a position of authority over the team.

Authority is particularly important in teams that have strong hierarchies within them, such as a cockpit crew. The team members who are lower in the hierarchy must have the option of going to someone with greater authority outside the team if there are concerns about a particular member of higher rank. That the leaders have authority over all team members should be built into the construction of the teams themselves.

Understanding Constraints, Problems, and Resources

This role is that of linking pin. If the leader plays this role properly, he or she enables the team members to understand their context as much as possible—ensures that the team members remember that they are operating within a larger context and what that context means to them in terms of task completion.

Identifying where the team may run into trouble during task completion and then providing assistance in getting the team through or around these problem areas is a useful role for team leaders. This "trouble" may come in the form of administrative or bureaucratic bottlenecks (for example, inability to obtain permission to build on a lot will preclude the house-building team from even beginning its work). It may come in the form of too few resources (for example, expertise needs to be brought in to complete a project, but no money has been budgeted for that expertise). It may come in the form of unforeseen disasters (for example, a blizzard may slow down or even stop a transportation team from getting goods from point A to point B).

The more the leader can foresee and help the team plan for potential problems and constraints, the better off the team will be. It will be less likely to view a problem as a highly unexpected and negative setback. It will view problems and getting around them simply as part of the work that must be accomplished. The better the team understands the resources it has available, the better it will recognize what it can and cannot accomplish.

Planning and Organizing Tasks

This is much more of a hands-on role than the other roles discussed thus far. Some teams may find that they do not want or need assistance in planning and organizing their work. In fact, the more autonomous the team, the more it will perceive any action of this type on the leader's part as meddlesome and over-controlling. This does not mean that all teams are able to plan and organize their tasks. When they first start up, most teams need at least some direction on which of the multitude of tasks they are to accomplish are most important for the organization. The leader may be an invaluable source of information in helping the team prioritize its tasks.

For many team leaders, recognizing when to become actively involved in the planning and organizing of team tasks is a problem. They don't know when they should take a more hands-on role with the team and when they should not. In this regard, teams must take the lead in interacting with their leaders. Team leaders must be able to cope with the fact that they may be needed by a new team just starting up but that later that very same team will not want their help any more. Although some team leaders may find this shift disconcerting, those who know about the rest of the list of roles discussed in this chapter will be glad to be rid of at least one!

A good rapport between the team and its leader is needed in order for a smooth transition from a hands-on to a hands-off approach. To have teams that work effectively and leaders who can make the transition from a controlling role to a coaching role, an organization needs to recognize that specific training for the leaders is necessary to deal with this sometimes ego-deflating experience.

Coordinating Work Activities

This role is related to the previous role; that is, it is closely associated with the traditional supervisory hands-on role. The leader can take on two "coordinating" roles: one is coordinating the tasks within the team itself, and the other is coordinating the team's overall efforts in the context of the larger organizational picture.

Coordinating the team's overall efforts from an internal perspective means that the leader will assist the team in allocating among members tasks to be done at specific times. However, to the extent possible, team leaders should try to avoid this type of coordination. If teams ask for help in making sure that all tasks are covered, then the leader may rightfully step in and suggest ways to allocate and coordinate work. But in the long run, it is more helpful to a team if the leader avoids this kind of involvement; instead, the leader may want to facilitate the first few sessions where the team members themselves work through this process and learn to take charge of it themselves.

Coordinating the team's overall efforts from an external perspective is a different matter. Here, the leader must have contact both with other units or teams that provide needed information, supplies, or services to the team, and with those that receive the team's outputs, be it information, supplies, services, or something else. This role requires that the leader know what is going on in many other parts of the organization so that the team gets what it needs when it needs it. The leader must help to ensure that the team provides its outputs in a timely manner so that the other parts of the organization are not held up in their work.

Organizations that are functionally differentiated (for example, marketing, manufacturing, sales, and so on) will know how important it is for someone to play this role. Often team members are too busy with their own work to keep track of how their team's work will be affected by and will affect other teams. By playing this coordinating role, leaders can make a big difference in ensuring that organizations made up of teams run smoothly.

Context and Team Success

The importance of the variables discussed in this chapter should not be underestimated. Teams that are not functioning well can trace many of their problems to the context in which they operate. Ensuring that the context is supportive to teams will dramatically increase the likelihood that teams will function well.

By using the items discussed in this chapter as a guide, an organization can evaluate its support of its teams. In the descriptions of each item, there are ideas for how to go about effecting changes to make the organization more supportive of teams.

The ramifications for organizations wanting to move into a team environment become clear in this chapter. It becomes obvious that team-based organizations are not created overnight. They come about only with the overall alignment of many other organizational systems. Team-based organizations function well only if the team leaders' roles and expectations are clear. Although dealing with the contextual variables takes time, effort, and resources, organizations need to be clear on them before engaging in the team-building process if there is to be a supportive context for teams. In turn, a supportive context contributes mightily to team success.

CHAPTER FIVE

TEAM CHARACTERISTICS

Both in research and in practice, certain team characteristics have been found to be of central importance in predicting team success. This chapter focuses on characteristics that describe the collective of the team; the characteristics of individual team members will be dealt with in the next chapter. The characteristics described in this chapter are *goal clarity and adoption, role clarity,* and *team efficacy.*

Goal Clarity and Adoption

The importance of goals and their relation to group performance has been recognized for decades (for example, Zander & Medow, 1963; Zander & Newcomb, 1967; Cartwright & Zander, 1967). A review of recent academic studies demonstrates that researchers often look for a high number of common goals as a prerequisite to high levels of team performance (for example, Eby & others, 1998; McClough & Rogelberg, 1998). Helping teams to set their goals is one of the most effective interventions a coach or facilitator can use in team building.

The critical role of goals was addressed in earlier chapters. Specifically, in order for the team to determine realistically the resources it will need, it must know its goals (Chapter Three). In addition, the organization must be clear on its own goals so that teams can effectively align their goals with those of the organization (Chapter Four). At the team level, all members must be fully informed of the team's goals and understand them. Otherwise, when team members disperse and go to work individually, the finished products each one brings back to the team may very well differ from what the other members were expecting.

It is not enough, though, for members to know the goals of the team. They must *adopt* the goals. Adopting goals can be a tricky issue, because members may have personal goals that are at odds with those of the team. Therefore, including all team members in the process of setting team goals is an effective means to accomplish the end of goal clarity and adoption by all members.

There are things *not* to do in this regard. For example, over the past several years, many organizations have subjected their employees to something called *strategic change*. In going through the change, the goals of the organization are frequently reset by a select few and handed off to the rest of the employees to be adopted and implemented. No voice is given to employees in the decision-making process. These strategic changes often are not looked upon favorably, may be ignored completely, and may even be subverted by the employees.

The primary problem with this type of organizational change process, noted in the organizational justice literature, is that it disenfranchises employees (for example, Bies & Shapiro, 1988). These changes are likely to fail to bring about the desired competitive advantage sought by engaging in the change process in the first place.

Involving the Team in Setting Goals

It does seem to be important for all team members to have a say in the goals of the team. Interestingly, if a team is asked what its goals are there often are as many different responses as team members themselves, unless the team has actually sat down together to set its goals. Setting team goals as a team can be a time-consuming process, but it is well worth it in the end. One of the reasons is simply informational. That is, team members know and understand the purpose of each goal because they were part of the decision-making process. Instead of questioning why they are doing certain activities, all of the team members know the answer, and the team saves time in the long run. If there are multiple steps to be taken in accomplishing the goal, all the members know the appropriate sequencing. For example, including all team members as part of the resource planning exercise, a long and drawn-out task (outlined in Chapter Three), can save lots of time later because all members know what is to be done, by when, and by whom.

Setting goals as a team also gives members a chance to vocalize which team goals are important to them individually. Even if a member does not agree with a goal that finally is adopted, at least that member understands why the goal was determined to be important and how that determination was made—and had ample opportunity to voice any concerns. In this way, team goal setting assists in getting all team members to adopt the goals.

Goal-Setting Preexercise

The following three questions can be used as a simple but effective way of diagnosing the extent to which teams have set goals and members have adopted them. Teams can do this exercise with one member—or the team leader—acting as facilitator. Alternatively, a facilitator can be brought in from outside to assist the team in working through these questions (as well as the others that follow in this chapter).

1. What are this team's goals?
2. How well does each team member understand the team's goals?
3. To what extent are the team's goals adopted by all of its members?

If goal setting is going to be used as part of a team-building process, the facilitator should ask these questions of each team member individually *before* embarking on a team goal-setting intervention. The reason this process works is that team members are quite competent at recognizing when they have no goals, unclear goals, or unrealistic goals, and at judging the extent to which team members adhere to the goals. Team members provide a lot of extremely useful information when answering these open-ended questions. The facilitator gets a quick understanding of what the team is working toward. Also, problems the team is experiencing often come out immediately when the responses to these questions are examined. Finally, the facilitator can become aware of any team members who may possibly be disruptive.

Even a well-functioning team needs to meet on a regular basis to discuss its goals. Change is the normal operating environment for teams, and team members need to keep abreast of any changes and how these changes affect the team's goals and performance. Change may come in a variety of ways: for example, the organization's market may change, the organization itself may change, or the members of the team may change. If members do not sit down regularly to discuss where they are in terms of goal accomplishment, future goals, and goal shifting, then they become disconnected and will begin to act like individuals rather than like members of a team. The team's effectiveness will thus begin to erode.

Role Clarity

One interesting aspect of team performance that seems to have been largely overlooked by many researchers as well as practitioners is role clarity. This phenomenon is somewhat surprising given that role conflict and role ambiguity are very familiar concepts to most human resource practitioners. In fact, close examination of an employee's role to determine if there is role conflict (conflicting requests from more than one source) or role ambiguity (uncertainty on the employee's part about what exactly is expected) is often used as a diagnostic tool when attempting to determine causes of poor job satisfaction among individuals. Just as with individuals, problems of role conflict and role ambiguity in teams may have far-reaching negative consequences.

Conflict in Roles

There is a high probability that roles will conflict in teams. The reason for this is fairly straightforward. Most team members are individual workers as well as members of teams. Some employees may even be members of several teams. For example, in a successful management consulting firm there are likely to be several projects running simultaneously. The same employee may be the leader of one project, a data analyst on another, a proposal writer on another; she may also be part of an internal team on employment equity. At any given time, this worker will have to decide where to expend her energy. It is entirely possible that overlapping team meetings may be scheduled and she will be able to attend only one of them. The result is a high degree of role conflict for this individual. This conflict also puts a high level of stress on the members of all the teams on which she has a role, stress that will be compounded if other members of a team are also on multiple teams.

Particular care needs to be taken to structure teams to avoid this kind of confusion. High expectations might inadvertently cause individuals to participate in too many projects or volunteer to be on too many teams. The result is that both the individual and the team perform poorly.

Ambiguity in Roles

Role ambiguity is also a potential source of problems for team members. The key here is to ensure that all members of the team know how their individual work fits into the team's common work. It is not unusual for teams to set goals but forget to assign individual tasks to team members; work may be duplicated (or "triplicated" or even "quadruplicated") because tasks have not been assigned to individual members. The team must establish clear expectations of what each individual must do and by when. Again, although this process may seem to be tedious and time consuming, it is important for the smooth functioning and success of the team. Ultimately, it avoids wasting time and has a positive effect on long-term team effectiveness.

There is another potential source of role ambiguity. If roles are not clearly designated, routine work may be "assigned" by default. For example, if one or two individuals usually do routine tasks they may be expected always to do those tasks, and feelings of inequity and unfair treatment may arise. Tasks should not be taken on by chance. Instead, the organization should insist that clearly defining member roles and expectations be part of any team-building process.

In contrast, role clarity has several upside potentials. When members are clear about their roles, it is obvious to all team members who is doing what. All members are aware of any time constraints involved in goal achievement, and all are in agreement regarding the schedule for completing their tasks. There is equity in workload distribution (both type and amount) over time. For example, one individual may do more on one project and less on another, or one person may do the routine work on one project and another person on the next project. Explicitly dividing up the work tasks ensures that all members of the team are involved in the work. Dividing up the work so that it will play to individual team members' strengths ensures that the team is efficient in its work distribution. All of these upside gains provided by role clarity can be had for very little time cost to the team.

Role Clarity Preexercise

Similar to the goal-setting exercise, the following open-ended question is an effective way for a facilitator to gain insight into the team's role clarity before any team building begins: "What is each team member's role in accomplishing the team's goals?" Responses to this question usually are an excellent source of information for the facilitator. By comparing the responses of each individual team member before entering the team-building situation, the facilitator has an excellent handle on how well the team is functioning.

Team Efficacy

A team's sense of its efficacy can be defined as its belief that it can successfully execute the tasks it sets out to accomplish. This is a necessary condition for the team to perform. The construct of team efficacy has been given a number of names, including *group efficacy, collective efficacy, self-efficacy for teamwork, group aspirations,* and *potency.* All amount to basically the same thing: the team's belief in itself to accomplish its work. Although *potency* (Guzzo, Yost, Campbell, & Shea, 1993) is the term used and measured most frequently in the academic literature to capture this phenomenon, I have found that the term *team efficacy* is intuitively easier for teams in organizational contexts to understand and appreciate.

Team Efficacy and Self-Efficacy

The central role that team efficacy plays in subsequent team performance can be explained by the well-regarded theory of self-efficacy developed by Albert Bandura (1977). In this theory, Bandura argues that self-efficacy is the "belief in one's capabilities to organize and execute the courses of action required to produce given attainments" (Bandura, 1977, p. 3). Self-efficacy has been demonstrated in many studies to have direct effects on performance (for example, Bandura, 1986) as well as indirect effects on performance through goal choice and goal commitment (for example, Locke & Latham, 1990). Given the importance of self-efficacy on performance at the individual level, it is not surprising that a similar variable would play an important role in team performance.

Team efficacy is distinct from self-efficacy. That is, the level of team efficacy is not determined by simply adding together the individual members' levels of self-efficacy. The types of tasks that teams are engaged in are qualitatively different from the types of tasks in which individuals are engaged. Successful accomplishment of team tasks requires first that the team believe that it can indeed accomplish those tasks.

Despite the appropriateness of team efficacy as a variable in any model of team performance, only recently have academic studies using team efficacy begun (for example, Kline & MacLeod, 1997; McClough & Rogelberg, 1998). In practice, team efficacy has yet to be tapped in any substantial manner.

Team Efficacy Preexercise

A set of eight items (Exhibit 5.1) developed by Guzzo, Yost, Campbell, and Shea (1993) to measure potency—"a collective belief in a group that it can be effective" (p. 87)—are the ones I have used (with slight modification) to assess team efficacy, as shown in Exhibit 5.1.

It should be noted that items 3 and 8 relate to what individuals outside the team think of the team. Outsider opinion is an important aspect of potency as described by Shea and Guzzo (1987b). That is, the team's sense of efficacy is determined partly by what others believe the team can do.

Sports teams, as well as individual athletes, have long known and capitalized on this. They "psych out the opposition" to give themselves a competitive advantage in winning. Although the typical organizational team probably won't be

EXHIBIT 5.1. MEASURING TEAM EFFICACY.

Team members first complete the items on their own. Then bring the team together to see how closely perceptions of team efficacy match among members. Discuss any differences of opinion and come to a consensus on the ratings for each item. Total the scores on the eight items to interpret the results. Interpretation of the scores is provided after the items.

	Completely disagree	Disagree somewhat	Neither agree nor disagree	Agree somewhat	Completely agree
1. This team has confidence in itself.	1	2	3	4	5
2. This team believes it can produce high-quality work.	1	2	3	4	5
3. This team expects to be known as a high-performing team.	1	2	3	4	5
4. This team feels it can solve any problem it encounters.	1	2	3	4	5
5. This team believes it can be very productive.	1	2	3	4	5
6. This team can get a lot done when it works hard.	1	2	3	4	5
7. No task is too tough for this team.	1	2	3	4	5
8. This team expects to have a lot of influence.	1	2	3	4	5

Note: Scores of 16 or less indicate a low level of team efficacy. Scores between 17 and 31 indicate moderate levels of team efficacy. Scores of 32 or more indicate a high level of team efficacy.

Source: Guzzo, R. A., Yost, P. R., Campbell, R. J., & Shea, G. P. "Potency in Groups: Articulating a Construct." *British Journal of Social Psychology, 32,* 98, 1993. Reproduced with permission.

engaged in psyching out anyone in particular, it must nevertheless be seen by others as capable.

Increasing Team Efficacy

Where does a team's sense of efficacy come from, and how can it be increased? These questions have not been answered fully. Nevertheless, some suggestions should be of assistance to practitioners (Bandura, 1977; Lindsley, Brass, & Thomas, 1995). First, encourage the team members to compare their performance with that of other teams. Second, increase the level of influence the team actually has. Third, improve on the degree of success the team has had in the past. Finally, ensure that team members know one another's capabilities.

Based on these suggestions, a facilitator can plan team efficacy interventions. A team that has been around for a period of time may have low levels of team efficacy. A team that is just starting up may report low or questionable levels of team efficacy. These two forms of low team efficacy call for unique forms of intervention.

For both types of low-efficacy teams, constructive feedback by an external person—someone who is in a position to judge the team's work and whose opinion the team values—is usually the most helpful intervention. This feedback should include an assessment of how well the team is accomplishing its goals, provide suggestions for ways in which the team can better achieve its goals, and offer ideas for shifting the team's goals to align them better with the organization's goals. Feedback of this type should be given very frequently to low-performing or newly started teams. Teams report that this type of feedback is highly desirable. They usually accept it and use it to begin working more effectively. As soon as they work more effectively, they accomplish more and begin to be successful. This feeling of success, then, breeds a higher level of team efficacy.

When a team that has been in existence for some time rates itself low on team efficacy, an examination of *why* the team is not accomplishing its goals is one of the first places to look. It may be that the team is lacking resources (physical, financial, human, or time), that one or more members are not contributing to or even are sabotaging the team's work, that members do not understand what the organization expects of the team, or that the team has set goals that are impossible to accomplish and its members are simply overwhelmed.

Other places to look for the reason behind low efficacy are in the clarity of the members' roles and the distribution of the team's work. It may be that members are unclear about what is expected of them, that they have too many other tasks interfering with their work on the team, or that they feel the assignment of tasks among team members is unfair. It is important in the diagnosis to have an open discussion with the team about what problems it perceives it has in getting its work done.

In addition to speaking with the team as a whole, it is important to speak with each member individually; there may be interpersonal reasons why the team is not performing and a group discussion would be detrimental to the team. The focus of the diagnosis should be on why work, tasks, or goals are not being accomplished. Keeping the focus "on task" will ensure that solutions relate to goal accomplishment and not something else. Teams may be able to diagnose themselves if they are able to keep themselves problem-oriented. If not, then the diagnosis is best made by someone external to the team.

A team facilitator or team leader should assess a team's efficacy at regular intervals. Regular assessment is particularly important with teams that are having trouble. The sooner low team efficacy is diagnosed, the better, so remedial action can be taken as soon as possible. Once the remediation takes place, watching low efficacy turn to high efficacy is highly reinforcing for a team.

With new teams, it is almost always valuable for a facilitator to spend time assisting them in making sure that their goals are challenging but doable and aligned with the organization's expectations. Celebrating and publicly recognizing early goal accomplishment is a well-known way to get teams to feel successful. Giving the team an identity (a name) makes it feel distinctive from the rest of the organization. In addition, when teams are just starting up, it is very useful to help them learn to articulate and clarify each member's role. In so doing, the team learns to determine which tasks make up each goal and how to allocate the workload in an effective way.

Most teams just starting up cannot compare themselves with other teams, have no influence, and have no past successes on which to build. These are three of the suggested ways to increase team efficacy. The fourth way, however, is one that should be implemented as soon as possible: members should learn each other's capabilities. An exercise that encourages this is to have members introduce themselves and tell about what knowledge, skills, and abilities they have that are related to the team's work. Keeping track of this information on a flip chart will show the team in a very concrete way that its collective set of skills is very strong.

Going through this exercise will help the team appreciate the unique contribution each member can make toward the team's goals. It will assist the team later on, allowing members to know in advance that the team may not have a particular skill needed to accomplish a goal and therefore will need to set about obtaining that skill. In addition, if a team member is having difficulty with a task and knows that another team member can help out, he or she is more likely to seek intrateam assistance.

The following case study offers the example of three teams that were just starting up in an organization. The case study demonstrates how one can increase team goal clarity, individual role clarity, and team efficacy in a workshop setting. This approach can be used by the team—designating a member as facilitator— or an outside facilitator can be brought in to assist.

Case Study: Goal Setting, Role Clarity, and Team Efficacy Interventions

A very large organization with multifunctioning sets of employees was introducing the team approach to a small group of employees in order to see how well it would work in the entire organization. One constraint was that the team building was to be done in a single day.

When I was asked to design the workshop, I decided that the focus of the day would be on setting team goals, clarifying roles, and introducing participants to team efficacy. I chose to focus on these three things because one day is a short period of time to work with teams, and these are the skills most likely to help newly formed teams get going.

Goal-Setting Intervention

After a brief introductory lecture describing my model of team performance, I told the teams that the rest of the day would be spent on aspects of the team characteristics part of the model. This approach played well to the needs of these team members; they had just recently been called "teams," had been given only very vague goals to accomplish over the next year, and were not sure about what they were to do next.

The employees who made up the teams were from three different areas of the organization. Two other facilitators and I broke them up into their teams and set to work. The first question that they needed to discuss among themselves and come to agreement on was this: "What is our long-term goal?"

This long-term goal question tended to fall into the category of a strategic problem because there were many alternatives, multiple constituents (often with conflicting interests), far-reaching ramifications, and no obvious "right way" to proceed. Thus, the question was difficult for some of the teams to answer. It was actually easier for them to answer the question when it was rephrased in the following manner: "What will the outcome of our work look like a year from now?" In general, it seems easier for individuals, as well as teams, to focus on a tangible product as a long-term goal in order to facilitate the process and move to the next step.

Facilitators kept track of what team members said throughout this long-term goal-setting process. The issues and concerns they raised and potential roadblocks were noted. What each member felt to be important was noted as well. We did this because when the teams assessed how they were doing six months later, it would be helpful for them to have notes about what their thinking was at the time. The team members appreciated this because they had a lot of other work on their plates and they knew how easy it would be to forget why a particular course of action had been taken earlier. Another reason for recording this information was that if the membership of a team changed, the recorded information about the team's goals could be provided to any new members.

Once the main goal was agreed on, the next step was to articulate the secondary goals. This process was fairly easy because the issues at this point focused on the tactical questions of what tasks needed to be done and in what order, and they sprang from the just-agreed-on long-term outcomes.

It is essential that the outcomes of the secondary goal-setting process be noted (flip charts are helpful tools here), much as they were in the long-term goal-setting process. Each secondary goal and the time at which it is expected to be completed must be noted. It may be necessary to break down the secondary goals further into tertiary goals.

By this time—about midday—the teams all had gained a tangible outcome from the workshop so far. Their long-term goals had been stated, and their secondary and tertiary goals and time lines associated with them had been planned. This was very useful, especially in making sure that the teams would be willing to participate fully in the afternoon's activities. To come next was the assignment of who would do what.

Role Clarity Intervention

Once the long-term goal had been set and the secondary and tertiary goals discussed and scheduled, it was time to set the roles and become clear on each member's contribution. Although the long-term goal was known to be the responsibility of the entire team, the secondary and tertiary goals (often termed *tasks*) were assigned to particular team members as their own responsibilities. Teams did this by naming the task and having one member agree to be responsible for its accomplishment. In most cases, members volunteered because they had either the expertise or the time to do the work.

Depending on the nature of the team, tasks can be allocated on a volunteer basis or by a supervisor. The members of these teams knew one another well and were all present at the time of the task allocation. However, if teams are geographically dispersed or team members do not know each other's skills but need to be up and running immediately, then task assignment by a supervisor may be more appropriate. Regardless of how tasks are allocated, because the allocation is done up front and publicly, team members all know what each member contributes to the overall goal. It is at this stage that any "social loafers"—those team members who allow the rest of the team to do all the work while they take credit for the result—are made obvious to the rest of the team.

A quick aside here about social loafers. Team members have some discretion over how social loafers are treated at the role-allocation stage in the team-building process.

If someone is not doing his fair share, the team members may pressure him to take on more responsibility. However, it is sometimes the case that the team needs help with social loafers. The person to whom the team reports needs to intervene with the social loafer and ensure that he starts carrying his fair share of the workload. This intervention is perceived by the team to be one of the critical roles of the team leader (see the section on "Dealing with Team Conflict" in Chapter Four).

At the workshop, once tasks were allocated, the team members discussed any potential scheduling issues or expertise needs they were going to have in trying to achieve their secondary or tertiary goals. We did this because a team member foresaw needing to call on another team member for specific help; he knew that a particularly busy time of year was coming up. He needed help to accomplish his allocated task. Other team members used this information to determine who could provide help and when.

This exercise in role clarity is particularly useful if secondary goals are to be accomplished in parallel. It is imperative that teams do not overwhelm each other with requests to accomplish all of their secondary goals at the same time. It is also helpful to go through this exercise because there may be organizational level activities and schedules that need to be taken into account by teams when scheduling their own work. If teams are composed of individuals from different functional units, the functional unit schedules may put additional scheduling constraints on a team's work.

The teams were required to codify the information they had gained at the goal-setting and role-clarification workshop. The information then was to be disseminated to all team members to post visibly at their workstations. It was agreed that team members could call meetings when they needed help accomplishing their goals, when they accomplished their goals, when there needed to be goal-schedule revisions, or when there were goal shifts (for example, secondary goals added, taken away, or modified). It was also agreed that each team would meet in a specified period of time to review goals, determine if they were on schedule, and discuss any issues that needed to be dealt with by the team as a whole. One member was designated to call and set up the meeting.

Team Efficacy Intervention

The next step for the teams was to gain a "can-do" attitude. Because they were just starting up, the teams did not have high levels of efficacy.

Each team member spoke individually about their knowledge, skills, and abilities (see the earlier section in this chapter on "Increasing Team Efficacy"). One of the team members was assigned to record the information on the flip chart. This information was subsequently typed up and sent around to the teams.

The teams agreed that the goal-setting and role allocation information would be made into a wall-size sheet where goal accomplishments could be publicly noted. When the set goals were attained, this information would be made known to the rest of the organization through the company newsletter. The teams agreed to celebrate their accomplishments by hosting potluck lunches and inviting the team leaders to join.

Last, the teams gave themselves names so that they were distinguishable from the rest of the organization. The products or services they were responsible for would then be easily attributed to the correct team. Each team as a unit could be recognized by the rest of the organization. This is often a fun way to end a busy and demanding day. Because the participants have been through the process of setting goals, allocating who is going to do what, and getting to know one another, they have some good ideas about what they want to be called. It is frequently the case that they will start using their team name to call meetings, refer to their work, and so on. All of this contributes to a high level of team efficacy.

Although this exercise was the last for the day for these teams, there was much that the organization could still do to increase the level of efficacy of its teams. Some suggestions were to allow successful teams to have a say in decisions made at higher levels in the organization. Another was to have highly placed individuals publicly recognize the work of the teams.

At the end of the workshop, although tired, the team members had accomplished a great deal for themselves. They were ready to work and they were likely to be successful in meeting their goals.

Characteristics of Successful Teams

The team characteristics described in this chapter are those that I recommend organizations seek to attain first when trying to get their teams to be more effective. The reasons for this are several. First, goal clarity and adoption, role clarity, and team efficacy have been found to be strongly related to team performance. Second, the interventions associated with these variables are not nearly as costly to the organization as some of those presented in earlier chapters, which include overhauling the performance reward system. As a result, management is more likely to accept and fund team characteristic interventions as part of team building. Third, these variables have a high degree of "face validity" to team members. That is, most team members respond positively to focusing on the goals of the team, the roles of the team members, and team efficacy. They do not usually want to talk about interpersonal problems; they want to find out how to work more effectively.

Finally, in the workshop modules based on these variables, teams actually set goals for themselves, define their individual roles, and discuss ways to increase and recognize their team efficacy, and they do so in the context of their organizations. As a result, they walk away with something they can use. Thus, team members usually see immediate value because they put what they have learned into practice.

CHAPTER SIX

MEMBER DISPOSITIONS

Most of us have had the opportunity to work on teams in which we did not like at least one other member. On many teams, the members barely know one another's names when they meet to do their work. Yet usually these teams get their work accomplished. Team members do not have to like each other to work well together.

However, a number of team-building facilitators continue to focus on team members' individual differences as the basis for their interventions. The assumption underlying this approach is that "personality clashes" are the primary reason why teams do not perform as well as they should. As exercises, personality inventories are often completed by team members and the results shared with the group. The utility of this approach is suspect, and organizations should be wary of facilitators who base their interventions on such personality inventories (for example, Luft, Kingsbury, & Schrader, 1990; Reddy, 1994).

Sometimes the team is taken away to engage in some form of recreational activity. These activities—such as mountaineering or white-water rafting—usually incorporate some element of fear so that a bonding experience will supposedly take place. Certainly there are instances when a boot-camp experience can make team members bond more tightly; if so, this is a functional exercise for the team. Military teams are a good example; team members must feel some level of responsibility toward the well-being of their fellow members. But the success of this type of intervention within the organizational contexts that most teams operate in has yet to be demonstrated.

These member-focused approaches stand in stark contrast to the team-building interventions that most organizations need in today's workplace, which were discussed in the previous chapters and will be addressed further in the next chapters. Specifically, this book assumes that if the team has no focused goals, is unclear about the members' roles, has too few resources to work with, and has no supportive context in which to operate, it simply will not make a whit of difference if the team members are a close-knit bunch.

But the question remains as to whether some individual differences really do matter in team performance. That there is little evidence to support this idea means one of two things: either there really are no individual differences that matter, or there are individual differences that do matter but they have not been identified yet. I take the latter position. My position is based primarily on my interactions with team members themselves. When the team members like one another or have some sort of chemistry, they *do* seem to be more productive than if they are all squabbling.

The rest of this chapter will be devoted to providing some evidence to support the notion that at least a few individual characteristics do matter to team performance. These few are *team-player ability, cooperativeness, team-player style,* and *personality traits.*

Team-Player Ability

The first individual characteristic that has been demonstrated to be related to team performance is that of being a team-player as measured by the Team Player Inventory (TPI) (Kline, 1999b). My research using this ten-item inventory assesses the degree to which individuals are positively predisposed to working on teams (Kline & MacLeod, 1997; Kline, 1999b). The items on the TPI were designed based on the adage, "Past behavior is the best predictor of future behavior." More specifically, the items reflect individual perceptions about how team or group work in the past affected their performance and their desire to work on teams in the future. The TPI questionnaire is reproduced in Exhibit 6.1.

In my research program, I have found that the higher the scores on the TPI, the more effectively the team carried out its work processes—with one caveat. The relationship is not a direct one; that is, scores on the TPI were not *directly* related to work process effectiveness. Rather, scores on the TPI *moderated* the relationship between team characteristics and work process effectiveness. Figure 6.1 demonstrates this relationship. Basically, what this means is that if team characteristics are positive and team member scores on the TPI are high, the two factors will in-

EXHIBIT 6.1. THE TEAM PLAYER INVENTORY.

Each team member completes the TPI individually. The scores can be averaged across all members to provide a team TPI score.

Read each item and determine the extent to which you agree with the statement. Interpretation of the scores is provided after the items.

	Completely disagree	Disagree somewhat	Neither agree nor disagree	Agree somewhat	Completely agree
1. I enjoy working on team/group projects.	1	2	3	4	5
2. Team/group project work easily allows others *not* to "pull their weight." "R"	1	2	3	4	5
3. Work that is done as a team/group is better than the work done individually.	1	2	3	4	5
4. I do my best work alone rather than in a team/group. "R"	1	2	3	4	5
5. Team/group work is overrated in terms of the actual results produced. "R"	1	2	3	4	5
6. Working in a team/group gets me to think more creatively.	1	2	3	4	5
7. Team/groups are used too often when individual work would be more effective. "R"	1	2	3	4	5
8. My own work is enhanced when I am in a team/group situation.	1	2	3	4	5
9. My experiences working in team/group situations have been primarily negative. "R"	1	2	3	4	5
10. More solutions/ideas are generated when working in a team/group situation than when working alone.	1	2	3	4	5

Note: "R" denotes that the item is coded in reverse for scoring purposes.

Scores range from 10 to 50. A score of 20 or less indicates that the individual (or team if using an averaged score) is not predisposed to working on teams. A score between 21 and 39 indicates that the individual or team is generally ambivalent about working on teams. A score of 40 or more indicates that the individual, or team, is positively predisposed toward working on teams.

Source: Kline, T.J.B. "The Team Player Inventory: Reliability and Validity of a Measure of Predisposition Towards Organizational Team Working Environments." *Journal for Specialists in Group Work,* 24, 102–112, 1999. Reproduced with permission.

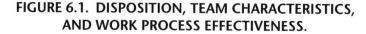

FIGURE 6.1. DISPOSITION, TEAM CHARACTERISTICS, AND WORK PROCESS EFFECTIVENESS.

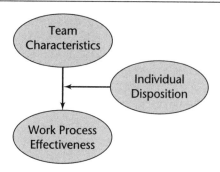

teract to have a positive effect on work process. If team characteristics are negative and member scores on the TPI are low, they will combine to produce a negative effect on work process effectiveness. When team characteristics are negative, however, high levels of TPI do not seem to be able to overcome the problem.

Thus, the research using the Team Player Inventory can be summarized by stating that the individual differences captured by the TPI measure does have some effect on teams' work process performance. However, the relationship is not strong.

Cooperativeness

The next individual difference that I have found in my research program to be positively related to work process effectiveness is cooperativeness (Kline, 1999a, 1999b; Kline & MacLeod, 1997; Kline, MacLeod, & McGrath, 1996; Kline & Sell, 1996). This work has been both qualitative and quantitative. In the Kline, MacLeod, and McGrath work, we asked seventy-five members of thirteen different teams from various organizations to tell us what they believed made them effective. Cooperation among team members was one of the more frequently cited items.

A seven-item measure of cooperativeness used in the quantitative studies (Kline & MacLeod, 1997; Kline & Sell, 1996) was based on the work of Johnson and Johnson (1983) and Johnson, Johnson, and Anderson (1983). These items were developed on the basis of group work in classroom settings, so the wording was changed to reflect a workplace setting. However, the reason these items are useful is that they are all oriented toward sharing work, sharing information, helping other employees, and learning. They are not the kind of broad-brush statements that are characteristic of many personality inventories.

As with the TPI measure, cooperativeness scores are not directly related to work process effectiveness but rather moderate that relationship, as shown in Figure 6.1. As on the TPI measure, scores on cooperativeness were measured at the individual team member level, and then scores were aggregated across members to arrive at a team score of cooperativeness.

One of the unexpected results of my research was that I did not find individual levels of competitiveness to be a negative influence on team performance (Kline & MacLeod, 1997; Kline & Sell, 1996). This finding may be explained somewhat by an examination of the constructs of cooperativeness and competitiveness. Although the two may intuitively seem to be polar opposites, when individuals complete inventories that assess both these traits they are actually unrelated to one another (Kline, 1995). In other words, individuals can be high in both cooperativeness and competitiveness, low in both, or high in one and low in the other. In addition, I found that, contrary to popular belief, women did *not* score higher in cooperativeness than men, and men did not score higher than women in competitiveness (Kline, 1995).

Team-Player Style

Parker's (1996) work with more than fifty team-oriented organizations suggests that there are four different types of personalities that contribute to team performance. He notes that each of the four types has something to contribute to the success of the team; conversely, each of the four types carried to its extreme is detrimental to the team. All team members have the capacity to use all four types, but any individual tends to use one type primarily. The four types are *contributor, collaborator, communicator,* and *challenger.*

The contributor is primarily a task-oriented individual. This team member is one who "enjoys providing the team with good technical information and data, does his or her homework, and pushes the team to set high performance standards and to use their resources wisely" (Parker, 1996, pp. 63–64). Contributors assist the team in setting goals, setting priorities, and solving problems, and do so in as efficient a manner as possible.

The collaborator is a goal-oriented person who is often described as having the big picture in mind. This member tends to focus on the vision and mission of the team and keeps the team on track and focused on its long-term goals. Other characteristics of collaborators are their willingness to pitch in and assist others, and even to work outside of their normal roles, to facilitate meeting the team's goals.

A member who is primarily a communicator emphasizes team process, defined by Parker as "how the team goes about completing its tasks and reaching its goals" (p. 75). Thus, individuals of this type are defined through their interpersonal processes as opposed to their work processes. The communicator, therefore, is concerned with listening, getting all members to speak up, resolving conflicts, building consensus, providing positive feedback, and building a supportive climate within the team itself. The communicator is convinced that the interpersonal "glue" between members is a primary contributor to the team's success.

Finally, the challenger is the team member who questions, disagrees openly with authority, and encourages the team to take calculated risks. Challengers are "candid, open, honest, and above all, deeply concerned about the direction of the team. And they very much want the team to succeed" (Parker, 1996, p. 80). Although challengers may seem to be a negative force on the team, they are not. They challenge decisions made and directions taken. They are not afraid to ask questions about why the team is proceeding with a particular course of action.

Parker's book includes an inventory that helps team players identify their own particular styles. Certainly, these four styles make sense and are reasonable. However, it would have been helpful if Parker had provided the research evidence that these four styles do indeed exist, to what extent they overlap, and to what extent each contributes to team performance.

Personality Traits

The Big Five personality traits have been demonstrated to exist through factor-analytic procedures dating back to the 1940s. These traits have been replicated using different populations, languages, and age groups, and using both self-assessment and peer evaluations (Hogan, 1992). The five traits are *agreeableness, conscientiousness, extroversion, neuroticism* (or, at the other end of the scale, *emotional adjustment)*, and *openness to experience* (Costa & McCrea, 1992). Importantly, these five personality characteristics have been shown to predict employee job performance (for example, Kichuk & Wiesner, 1998).

Despite the utility of the Big Five in predicting individual employee performance, there has been little evidence regarding the usefulness within the team performance context. Yeatts and Hyten (1998) reviewed the existing literature on this matter, and the bottom line is that the results are mixed. Some of the personality variables behaved as expected, some behaved unexpectedly, and most had no effect on team performance. Still, it is too early to dismiss the Big Five as useless, and therefore a description of each and how it is expected to be related to team performance follows.

Team members who have high scores on agreeableness, which is also termed *likability*, are courteous, flexible, trusting, good-natured, cooperative, forgiving, soft-hearted, and tolerant. The research evidence is equivocal with regard to this particular trait. On the one hand, high levels of agreeableness are presumed to be useful in developing group cohesion; on the other hand, if agreeableness is too high then members do not challenge ideas, goals, work processes, and so on, and it becomes easy to engage in "groupthink" (Janis, 1982). Groupthink occurs when the team's drive to be cohesive becomes more important than its drive to do the right thing.

A person who scores high on conscientiousness would be characterized as dependable, careful, responsible, organized, hardworking, persevering, and achievement-oriented. Obviously, members having high levels of this trait would be helpful to a team because they are likely to work hard at achieving the team's goals.

The team member who enjoys socializing, is gregarious and talkative, is assertive, and generally has a high energy level is likely to be high in extroversion. This team member ensures that there is interaction between team members. Too much interaction may be detrimental to the team because it takes the members away from the job at hand; however, with little or no interaction, team members would not be able to discuss their work. Thus, some extroversion is needed for teams to perform.

Neurotic team members are generally assumed to have a negative influence on team performance. Team members who are anxious, depressed, easily angered or embarrassed, highly emotional, and insecure will not easily adjust to the constant changes intrinsic to teamwork. In addition, these individuals make the interactions between team members difficult. The opposite end of this particular personality subscale—emotional adjustment—however, is assumed to be of particular value to teams that must operate in continually changing environments and deal with complex tasks and interactions. Thus, low scores on the neuroticism subscale are considered desirable for team performance.

The openness-to-experience trait is characterized by intelligence, imagination, curiosity, originality, broad-mindedness, and artistry. There is very little research examining this particular trait with regard to team performance. It seems reasonable to suggest, though, that if a team is required to generate ideas or think about ways to pursue unique alternative courses of action, then members with high levels of openness to experience would be useful to the team.

Member Characteristics: Common Themes and Implications for Practice

An examination of the preceding personality or disposition variables shows some common threads when it comes to the expectations of both researchers and practitioners about who will make a good team member. It seems that at least some level of being able to get along with others is needed to be a member of a team, as demonstrated by the inclusion of cooperativeness and agreeableness as important personality traits.

There is also a need for team members to accomplish their work. The conscientiousness and collaborator descriptors highlight the importance of this variable. There is also some consensus that interaction between team members is needed. This is facilitated by the extrovert or the communicator. There is also the caution that there must be some cooperative conflict in teams. That is, decisions made by the team need to be openly discussed, and the pros and cons of alternatives recognized. This is the role of the challenger and also the antithesis of high levels of agreeableness.

So how best to use this information in the team performance context? Part of the answer lies in the type of team one is talking about. Chapter Two described three main types of teams: crews, task forces, and standing teams. Depending on the work associated with these team types, different mixes of personalities need to come into play more often. Unfortunately, then, there is no one best answer about who makes a good team player. Instead, the answer is, "It depends."

For example, it will not matter much if team members on a crew get along with one another or if they have a lot of interaction. Their goals are so clear and their roles so well-defined that it is irrelevant to worry about interaction. However, the hierarchical nature of these crews means that a challenger personality is not needed and may be detrimental to the team's performance. In contrast, being highly conscientious and doing one's job well is essential to the functioning of crews.

When it comes to task forces, which typically are assigned some fuzzy long-term goal, it is likely to be important to involve individual members who can brainstorm lots of different ideas, challenge the alternative courses of action, and then keep the task force on track if the goal is a long-term one.

Probably more than other teams, standing teams need to be made up of members who get along with one another. Some of these team members are together for years at a time. Tolerating the idiosyncrasies of other members, ensuring that trust between members develops and is maintained, and a generally positive and upbeat attitude—these are all things that will help standing teams work well together over the long haul.

The Team Player Inventory and the findings associated with it suggest that team members, regardless of team type, who have had positive experiences working on teams in the past will likely be amenable to working on them in the future. Thus, organizations should look for individuals who are at least not negatively predisposed to teams if they value and expect teamwork.

In the future, the understanding of individual differences may have clear implications for the human resource systems of selection and training. At present, however, because the evidence regarding these variables is quite limited and the findings are mixed, caution should be exercised in trying to select employees with a particular team personality type. The overwhelming evidence demonstrates the obvious importance of the contextual variables discussed in earlier chapters. Thus, these are better places to intervene.

Nevertheless, if organizations have decided that they truly need to select employees with a team orientation, then some reasonable steps will help ensure that the selection procedure occurs in a rational and legally defensible manner. The first step is to understand clearly the tasks in which the teams are going to be engaged. The next step is to determine what particular personality characteristics would be most useful for that particular task. The final step, then, would be to find a reliable and valid way to evaluate an applicant's measure of the desired personality trait. Such an approach includes selecting a personality measure already in existence, creating a new organization-specific personality measure, or constructing interview questions that will get at the relevant personality characteristics.

The overriding concern here is that the personality characteristics be clearly linked to the performance of the team. This linking process requires some unique job-analytic skills: it is important to note not just the tasks associated with the team's job but also the means by which the team members interact to get the tasks accomplished. Although team task-analysis technologies are not yet perfected, work is being done on them (for example, Baker and others, 1998).

There is an added complexity when staffing existing teams. If a team needs to hire a new member, it may decide internally that the team would be best served by an individual whose personality characteristics will fill a gap on the team. For example, consider a team that is made up primarily of members who are hard-driving and achievement-oriented. That team may perceive that a member who encourages interpersonal interactions and assists in making the team's working climate more relaxed would be an asset at this point. The team's desires in the hiring process should be attended to by the human resource unit.

Team training using personality variables can be helpful in some instances, especially as an icebreaker for teams whose members do not know one another. Past that function, though, the use of personality-based training is not apparent. The reason is that, according to the standard assumptions of personality theory, personality is extremely difficult to change. For example, a team-building facilitator may point out that the team is missing a collaborator type, but this observation is not usually going to help the team when it goes back to work. No team member is likely to become a collaborator overnight, nor is the team likely to be provided the resources to hire a collaborator type.

In summary, although the hunt for a "team personality" that will make teams work has intuitive appeal, it is far more important to pay attention to the more substantive variables described earlier, such as providing the needed resources to teams, getting the organizational context to be supportive of teams, and helping the team clarify its goals, the roles of each member, and its team efficacy. There are also several other valuable interventions that will be addressed in the chapters that follow.

CHAPTER SEVEN

CONCEPTS OF WORK PROCESS EFFECTIVENESS

The term *work process* refers to how the team accomplishes its work, as opposed to tangible work outcomes. Two approaches for examining work process effectiveness of teams are presented in this chapter. The first is based on aspects of the models of team performance put forward by Hackman (1987, 1990), Hackman and Oldham (1980), and Sundstrum, DeMeuse, and Futrell (1990). The processes encompassed in this approach derive primarily from the human resource management perspective, and more specifically from the literature on job enrichment. That is, there is an implicit assumption that individual workers, and by extension, teams of individual workers desire enriched work environments (for example, Morgan, 1997, pp. 34–39). These are environments in which the individual or the team engages in important "whole" pieces of work, is autonomous, uses a high level of skill and a variety of skills to accomplish work, and receives accurate feedback about performance.

The second approach comes from a variety of research as well as the information I have gained from team members themselves. It is based on the decisions that get made as a team works, the methods for assessing work in progress, and the team's work performance standards.

The First Approach: Job Enrichment

Hackman and his colleagues have observed that certain variables affect the level of effort an individual worker is willing to put into a task. These same variables have been suggested also to affect the level of effort a team is willing to put into the task. The variables are based on the job enrichment work motivation theory and include the skill variety needed to complete the task, the importance of the task, the task as part of a larger whole, the feedback provided regarding task performance, and the autonomy associated with completing the task.

Although the rationale behind Hackman's approach (1987) is reasonable, until recently there has been little attempt to test this aspect of his model. In my work, I have found that both the organizational context (Chapter Four) and the team characteristics (Chapter Five) positively predicted how a team rated its work process effectiveness (Kline, 1999a). An eight-item work measurement of processes (see Exhibit 7.1) used in my study included items that reflected Hackman's model.

Most of the teams that have participated in my research want feedback on how their responses compare with other teams' responses on these items. Obviously, these measures hold a high degree of face validity for team members. Responses to these items provide a wealth of possible intervention information.

Job enrichment literature assumes that employees want enriched jobs. Yet research and ordinary observation both indicate that this is much too simplistic a view. Instead, different employees will desire different levels of enrichment in their jobs. Some employees just want to put in a nine-to-five day during which they are not called upon to do anything more than what they have been contracted to do and leave it at that. The same logic applies to teams and teamwork. One approach, suggested by Oldham, Hackman, and Pearce (1976), is that individual employees who have high levels of *growth need strength* will not respond as positively to job enrichment as those with low growth need strength. Growth need strength refers to an individual's desire to be challenged in his or her work such that personal growth results. The situation for teams is more complex because members may have varying levels of growth need strength. Furthermore, some of the empirical work has failed to find support for the notion of growth need strength (for example, Cherrington & England, 1980; Tiegs, Tetrick, & Fried, 1992).

Evaluating Desire for Enrichment

Given the limited support for the assumption that all teams want enriched work environments and the tenuous support for the growth need strength construct, a highly useful intervention when working with teams is to ask the teams not only

EXHIBIT 7.1. JOB ENRICHMENT EVALUATION.

All statements are rated *by the team as a unit*. Read each item and determine the extent to which the team agrees with the statement. Discuss the items that are rated as a 1 or a 2 within the team. Include in these discussions what alternatives the team has by which to improve the ratings on these items. Then meet with the team leader to discuss the team's concerns and suggestions.

	Completely disagree	Disagree somewhat	Neither agree nor disagree	Agree somewhat	Completely agree
Team Skills					
1. Team members are required to use a variety of skills for the team's work.	1	2	3	4	5
2. Team members are required to use a high level of skills for the team's work.	1	2	3	4	5
Work Importance					
3. My team's work has significant consequences for the organization.	1	2	3	4	5
Outcome Meaningfulness					
4. My team produces whole/meaningful pieces of work.	1	2	3	4	5
5. My team produces work with visible outcomes.	1	2	3	4	5
Team Autonomy					
6. My team is responsible for its work outcomes.	1	2	3	4	5
7. My team works autonomously.	1	2	3	4	5
Work Feedback					
8. My team receives accurate and timely feedback on its work.	1	2	3	4	5

to rate each item based on their *current* situation but also to rate each item based on their *desired* situation. The magnitude of the difference between the current and desired ratings will provide the facilitator with information on where best to intervene (if at all).

For example, the first two questions in the evaluation address skills. If the team rates the variety of skills currently needed to accomplish its work as a 1 and the desired level of skill variety as a 1, then there is not a problem. If, however, the team rates the variety of skills currently needed as a 1 and the desired level of skill variety as a 5, it may mean that the job is not challenging enough for the team. There is also a problem if the team rates the variety of skills currently needed as a 5 and the desired level of skill variety as a 1: it may mean that the team finds the job too challenging.

Going through these items one at a time using a current versus desired technique is a valuable exercise. It keeps the team facilitator from assuming there is a problem if there is not one, and it helps him or her to detect the most salient problems the team faces regarding job enrichment.

Increasing Job Enrichment

So how can a team increase its level of enrichment if that is desired? When it comes to skill enrichment, the tasks assigned to the team are highly relevant. If the team wants to use more varied skills or higher levels of skills, then it needs to lobby the organization to provide more complex work. On the flip side, team members must realize that they may not have the requisite skills for these new, complex tasks. Members should be prepared to take remedial action (for example, night school classes or training provided by the organization) to upgrade their skill levels.

As for the importance and meaningfulness of the team's work—addressed by the second two sets of items on the evaluation—these too must be improved by the types of tasks that the organization assigns to the team. Teams that want more of this kind of enrichment need to be prepared to propose redesigning their work. Such a redesign would include the team's having work that is readily visible to others as important, as well as seeing a piece of work completed from start to finish.

Autonomy is another important aspect of job enrichment. Team autonomy comes into play particularly in how the decisions for the team are made. Teams that make their own decisions need to be prepared to live with the consequences. Critical to the success of decisions is feedback to the team on its performance. Performance feedback will provide the team with the information it needs either to change direction or to continue on as it has been doing.

Of all the team interventions that adopt the job enrichment approach to making work processes more effective, the most important is to provide useful feedback. Telling the team how it is doing as it actually works will help guide the team in the right direction. The utility of the other job enrichment interventions is highly dependent on the nature of the team's tasks and the desires of the team members themselves.

The following case study describes a team enrichment intervention. However, it should be noted that a blanket suggestion to increase job enrichment for all teams is not yet warranted because there is simply too little evidence that enriched jobs are a good thing for all teams.

Case Study: Team Enrichment Intervention

In this nonprofit fundraising organization, an intense fundraising campaign occurs over a two-month period once a year. The organization employs approximately 250 individuals full-time. These employees are grouped together functionally and nominally are called teams.

The fundraising team is the largest in the organization, and many of its members are part-time. This team receives recognition from the newspapers, radio stations, all levels of government, and the private sector. In addition, the team as an autonomous unit plans the fundraising strategy, including devising slogans and posters for publicity. Its fundraising efforts are very successful. In other words, this team has a high degree of visibility and stature in the community, and its morale is quite high.

There are also several nonfundraising teams in the organization that make it possible for the organization to function on a year-round basis. These teams include those that distribute the funds raised to local agencies, monitor the spending of funds, and provide general administrative support within the organization. They are largely unknown to the public. They generally feel that their work is unrecognized and that they are the "unsung heroes" of the organization. They function under the direction of their supervisors in a traditional, hierarchical manner with little autonomy. Their morale is quite low.

In addition to the recognition and autonomy issues, the fundraising team's work has a set beginning and ending—a high-energy, intense, short period of time. The work of the other teams has no such cyclical nature. These teams do virtually the same type of work year-round. Thus, they have no sense of completion in their jobs. Although most jobs in general are noncyclical in nature, in this case a high level of social comparison goes on between the teams because they are part of the same organization and work out of the same office building.

The discrepancies in the types of work done by the different teams were causing the organization a lot of difficulty and hard feelings between employees. The job enrichment approach offers a useful perspective on the low morale of the nonfundraising teams and several solutions to the problem.

First, the issue of recognition needs to be dealt with. The organization needs to find ways to recognize as much as possible the important role within the organization of the nonfundraising teams. Highlighting that it could not function without them is one way to do this. External recognition of the type experienced by the fundraising team would be useful as well. For example, agencies that benefitted from the work of the nonfundraising teams could be solicited to provide feedback.

Second, the organization needs to think of restructuring the work of the nonfundraising teams into project-type pieces. Each project should be named, have a definitive starting point, include measures of success along the way, and have a definitive ending.

Third, as the projects are completed, they need to be formally recognized and publicized. This recognition should include a celebration of some sort, as well as acknowledgment by the fundraising team and by the organization's management of the importance of the work of the nonfundraising team.

Fourth, job enrichment when it comes to responsibility and autonomy is also needed. This issue should be dealt with primarily by the supervisor of each team, and the supervisors may need some help in doing this. It may be difficult for them to delegate decision-making authority to the teams because it has been a normal part of their jobs for so many years. Delegation takes practice. One obvious approach is to make the transition from supervisor-directed teams to team-directed teams a gradual one. Initially, the supervisor should be very involved and influential in the team's decision-making process. Many teams recognize that their supervisors know the politics of the organization and how to get things accomplished. As teams become more practiced in making decisions, they will gain confidence and skill. Later, supervisors may distance themselves by simply being present at team meetings and answering questions but not actively getting involved in the decision making. As the team becomes more and more autonomous in its decision making, supervisors can be available to attend team meetings as requested but otherwise leave the decision making up to the team.

Many teams appreciate the graded approach suggested here and discussed elsewhere (Wellins, Byham, & Wilson, 1991). Teams that suddenly find themselves having to make decisions and be responsible for their outcomes, when they have never done so before, often find the situation intolerable and feel resentful of their supervisors for leaving them out on a limb. In addition, the graded approach allows the supervisor and team to gain confidence over time in how the team makes decisions and carries out its work.

Fifth, feedback plays a critical role. As the nonfundraising teams begin to work by themselves, they will require a high level of information about whether they are doing the right things and how well they are doing those things. The feedback is most likely to come from the supervisor, but it can also come from other team members, coworkers, other teams, self-assessment procedures, clients, and other individuals outside the organization, such as suppliers or distributors. Feedback should be actively solicited and provided to the teams on a timely basis.

If these five suggested actions are taken, it will help to ensure that the nonfundraising teams feel that their work is valued and also provide them with a sense of autonomy. In turn, their perceptions of the fundraising team will be less negative. All three outcomes are advantageous to the organization as a whole.

The Second Approach: Decision Making

The approach suggested here is quite different from the job enrichment approach because it does not assume that all teams desire enriched work environments. However, the approach does assume that the team actively makes decisions about its work. It has been my experience that organizations are asking teams to act autonomously, to make their own decisions, and to take responsibility for those decisions. It should be noted, however, that if a team never or rarely makes decisions about how its work or tasks will get done, this section will be of little use.

The following sections are organized around eight questions that tap into the decision-making processes of the team. After each is presented in turn, the rationale of why it is important is described. A team's responses to these questions provide an excellent way to help diagnose why it may be making poor decisions.

Is the Team the Right Size to Make Decisions and Accomplish Its Work?

With the amount of downsizing that has occurred in organizations over the past years, many teams have found themselves understaffed. They are asked to accomplish the same amount of work as in the past, or even more work, but with fewer people. In contrast, some teams report that they are too large. Changing membership, difficulty in calling meetings because of so many different people's schedules, disseminating information in a timely manner to all members, and members not reading material before attending meetings are all typical problems of large teams.

How large should the team be? It should be as large as it needs to be to accomplish the work and no larger. Thus, again we find that the nature of the team's task is a primary factor in team performance, particularly when teams are faced with making decisions. Many teams operate in dynamic environments where decisions have to be reached quickly, and large teams are notorious for their slow-moving decision-making processes. In some situations, certain decisions have significant political ramifications that will be best served by painstakingly involving all stakeholders at the decision-making stage so that no one tries to sabotage the success of the decision once it is implemented; these teams by definition need to be large. Teams also may need to be large if the decision is a complex one where a lot of information is required. In such cases, a large team is more likely than a small team to contain within it the expertise to assist in making the decision.

Teams that are the right size for the task have a much better chance of making decisions appropriately than teams that are not. Teams that are too small will not have enough time or the right mix of skills to make an informed decision. If the team is too small, it needs to lobby immediately for a change in task complexity, magnitude, or both. Otherwise, the team is bound either to make poor decisions based on too little information or to take too long to make the decision; neither outcome is acceptable. Teams that are too large easily get off track and take a long time to reach a decision. If the team is too large, then members who have the most relevant decision-making skills to offer should be kept on the team and the others should bow out.

Do Team Members Have the Interpersonal Communication Skills Necessary to Accomplish the Team's Work?

For a team to make adequate decisions, it should have the input of all its members. However, individuals are highly variable in their communication skills. Team members with good oratory skills may sway the team on the basis of their speaking technique rather than on the content of their arguments. Members who are more reticent and not likely to speak out may have excellent points that the team does not consider. These situations will compromise the team's performance.

There should be some assessment of team members' communication skills; all members must be able to express their opinions adequately. Interestingly, I have found that team members have insight into their own levels of communication skill. For those who are not used to speaking in public or who are unsure of how to organize their thoughts and make them clear, team decision making can be an arduous task. The team leader or team members should identify those individuals for whom communication is not a strong suit and take remedial action to improve their skills.

Do Team Members Have the Task-Relevant Skills Necessary to Accomplish the Team's Work?

Any decisions made by the team will have ramifications for how its work gets accomplished. Teams should make decisions that play to the strengths of their members, not decisions whose implementation requires skills the members do not have. There is an obvious exception to this general principle. When a task force is formed solely to make recommendations to the organization, then the organization is supposed to find ways to implement the decisions. However, for standing or functional teams, the team itself is usually required to carry out the work. The exercise on articulating and documenting team members' skills (see the team efficacy intervention described in the case study in Chapter Five) will help the team make decisions that are within its skill boundaries.

Does the Team Allow for Diversity of Opinion?

It is important to note that diversity as I use the term in this decision-making context relates only to task-related attributes, such as the differences in knowledge, skills, and abilities members bring to the decision-making task. The list does not include relations-oriented attributes, such as gender, age, functional unit, hierarchical level, and other possibly politically charged attributes (for example, Jackson, May, & Whitney, 1995). I strongly believe, and have found, that staying task-focused is the most responsible way to deal with issues of diversity.

When teams are requested to make a decision, they usually must do so within a specified period of time. If the schedule is short, then the team will likely not have the luxury of asking all members for their opinions and discussing each one at length. However, when there is some time available, alternative courses of action should be examined—particularly when an issue is brought up and there are conflicting opinions about the direction the team should pursue. At this point the very best knowledge, skill, and ability should be brought to bear on the question at hand. The team should actively seek out varying opinions if there is time to do so—even to the point of consulting individuals outside the team. This process can quickly become extremely time consuming, and thus the team should be taught some techniques on how to carry out this process in a systematic, efficient manner. Chapter Eight describes in detail one particular decision-making tool I have used with several organizations.

Does the Team Assess Various Alternatives Before Accomplishing Its Work?

This question is related to the diversity question, but it examines in more detail exactly how much time the team devotes to each different opinion. Granted, a crew usually works under such tight time restrictions that the leader is expected to make the decision and the other members to follow suit. Task forces and standing teams, however, can take a more leisurely approach. Teams that carefully weigh the pros and cons of alternative courses of action are likely to have thought through the potential problems that any course of action may bring. If nothing else, taking the time to do this provides the team with some ammunition for selling its decision to outsiders. The team can actively say, "This is what we have chosen to do. We have thought through the alternatives, and although none is perfect, this is the one we choose, and this is why. . . ." If it sounds as though I am advocating for teams to assess alternatives systematically in making their decisions—I am.

Does the Team Have Teamwide Recognized Performance Norms?

Decisions around the norms of the team are almost always left up to the team itself. Even teams that operate in a traditional organizational structure have some latitude when it comes to how members are expected to perform within the boundaries of the team itself. The team members' expectations of one another regarding such seemingly incidental issues as attending team meetings or coming to meetings prepared to discuss an issue should be structured into the team from the very start. It is interesting how often these small issues can cause team members to dislike working together, even if the end result is an excellent one.

Norms, by definition, are the unwritten rules that govern people's social interactions—whether they be familial, societal, or work-related. Instead of leaving the rules unwritten, I am advocating that teams specify as many of the norms for performance as possible. Although articulating expectations to such a fine degree may sound overly structured, it is important to get the rules of the game established before the team members begin their work. I have seen that specifying expectations rarely hinders the team and usually helps it. Why? If norms are not spelled out, members are left to their own devices to figure out what is or is not acceptable to the rest of the team. It is better for the team to agree on a set of rules from the beginning than to try to bring a rogue member into line later on. The time that teams often save by engaging in this activity is worth the effort.

Some typical performance norms concern attendance at meetings, punctuality at meetings, participation at meetings, volunteering to do other organizational work that will take away from team activities, on-time completion of work, and degree of detail expected in work. This list is not comprehensive by any means; it is useful, though, as a point of departure for what teams value in their work processes and expect of their members. Once the team begins to reach agreement on these issues, it tends to generate a number of other performance norms specific to its own work context. The more these norms are spelled out, the more clearly each member will be able to discern how well he or she is following the rules.

Does the Team Assess Its Progress in Its Work Before Completion?

Work assessment may go through many avenues; feedback may come from leaders, coworkers, or clients. Unfortunately for many teams, feedback from outsiders is little or nonexistent. Some teams I have worked with cannot even identify who their leader is so that they can ask that person for feedback! This situation is a precarious one.

In such cases, the team should engage in the process of giving itself feedback. Self-feedback helps compensate for the—common—lack of leadership feedback and gives the team the opportunity to correct its problems before someone outside the team's unit or organization provides unsolicited criticism. To give appropriate self-feedback, the team needs to do two things: set its goals and subgoals, and regularly and frequently review the extent to which it is accomplishing those goals. The team should set goals and subgoals *before* starting its work. This process allows all members to be clear about the goals and time expectations, so they can be vigilant and proactive in providing feedback to the rest of the team.

Self-feedback needs to happen both regularly and frequently, it needs to be constructive and honest, and it needs to start early. If the team is not progressing toward its goals, it may need to make a change as simple as fine-tuning a work process to get itself back on track. Or, conversely, the team may have to rethink its entire approach to the problem. Without a feedback mechanism in place, though, the team will not be able to engage in either of these remedial actions because it won't recognize that there is a problem until it is too late.

Does the Team Allow for Modifications in Work Processes If Alternative Ways Are Suggested?

This last question follows up on the previous one. If the team receives feedback that it is not meeting its goals or expectations, then the team can decide to make some changes. Alternatively, even if the team is working well, some new way of adding value to the work may come along and the team may want to incorporate it. A decision to do nothing with the information is also a decision, but it does not require any action regarding modifying present work processes.

My advice is that teams should remain open to the possibility that there may be more effective or efficient ways to accomplish their goals. Even if the old way is functional, new technologies or personnel can provide an opportunity to streamline work. To even consider making the change, the team has to be willing to admit that the world is a dynamic place and that regularly changing the way work is carried out is now simply part of the work world. A team that is averse to assessing the utility of new work processes is likely to become dysfunctional, because teams need to keep current in the work processes they use. For example, if a surgical team does not put into practice the newest technology in keeping patients alive on the operating table, it is being negligent. Another example is if a marketing team is unaware of the potential of a new competitor, there may be disastrous consequences. Therefore, if a team does decide to consider alternative goals, alternative work processes, or some combination of the two, then the decision process begins once more.

The following case study exemplifies how best to use the decision-making approach in team interventions.

💾 Case Study: Team Decision-Making Intervention

Several student project teams were required to work together for the year, but initially their members didn't know one another. This teaching approach is very common in professional schools, where an incoming student class is divided into groups. The groups work together for a specified period of time (for example, a semester, two semesters, or even an entire year), during which time they are required to produce papers, work on case studies, build things, present business plans, and complete other such tasks. Usually these projects have substantive consequences for team members in that at least part of their grade depends on the team projects.

It is surprising how few professional schools provide team training in these situations. If one wanted to devise a way to help these student project teams get their work processes going effectively, the decision-making aspect is where the attention should be focused. Because the student teams are usually in a challenging and demanding environment, and because the students who pursue these kinds of degrees often have a high need for achievement, a job enrichment focus would be inappropriate. But many of these individuals have had little opportunity to work in teams before, and making decisions in a group setting does not come naturally to them. Therefore, focusing on decision-making skills is a fruitful way to address the work processes.

The steps in designing a decision-making work process enhancement workshop for students follow directly from the eight-question evaluation that I use with organizational teams. I recommend that the student teams meet for an entire day or two half-days to work through these questions one at a time. If they are told ahead of time that they will be provided with the tools that will facilitate their working together for the next several months, and that it is required that they attend and participate, then they actually will attend and the experience will help them to avoid many of the problems that are usually encountered by these types of teams.

The first question—regarding team size—is usually beyond the students' control; furthermore, these teams are usually designed to have three to six members and so are not large. We skip over this question. The next two questions ask the team members to talk about their own skills, both communication and task-relevant skills. These questions may be somewhat sensitive for team members, so a facilitator is appropriate for this particular team exercise. Even if the exercise is done with several teams in a large room, it still helps to have someone present directing the activity, handling questions, and keeping the work moving.

Team members who indicate that they have less than acceptable communication skills should be given instruction on how and what to read and practice on their own. Alternatively, or in conjunction with self-learning, a communication workshop can be set up to assist these students. A half-day workshop usually suffices to give the basics in communication skills, and it allows the students some time to practice the skills, which they can then bring to their teams. The workshop and referenced self-learning are relatively low-cost alternatives for the learning institution, and they pay back dividends: the teams become more functional almost right away.

The next question asks about task-related skills. This exercise is an important part of the decision-making process. The other members not only get to know and respect the skills of the other team members but also learn the strengths and weaknesses of the team as a whole. Project decisions they make can then emphasize the team's strengths and not require the team to produce something where the collective skills of the team are weak. If the team has the resources to secure outside assistance in areas where its skills are deficient (rarely the case with student project teams), then so much the better.

The fourth and fifth questions focus on the team's ability to come to a decision in the face of differing opinions. This activity is very difficult for most teams and really requires the team to have some sort of strategy at hand for making decisions. It is important to provide teams with at least one way to go through this decision-making task without getting bogged down literally for weeks, usually with infighting and hurt feelings as a result.

The next question, on norms for performance, also should be answered as a team exercise. The team members should discuss how they are to come together and what they expect of one another. The exercise is really a way to set up ground rules of conduct for the team. To overlook this activity is to invite problems later on, because each member may have a different perspective on how to interact. Getting the team members to agree to uphold the rules on such things as meetings, work quality, how they contact one another, when meetings get called, and so on, are excellent ways to get the team rolling. The teams can then proceed on their own to think up other ground rules specific to their membership and their project.

In an additional phase of the workshop, the teams are provided with the process and tools or mechanisms by which they will assess their work performance. It may be that this part of the workshop can come into play later as the teams begin to formulate what they will be doing for the term. Regardless of when it is done, a systematic process by which the teams learn how to assess themselves on a regular basis is invaluable.

Also during the workshop, the teams set their goals and subgoals, devise the tools they will use to determine how they are progressing toward those goals, determine how often they will be assessing themselves, and decide how the feedback on these assessments will be disseminated to the rest of the team. The more often the teams evaluate themselves, the better they will become at the process of self-assessment and the more clearly they will perceive the value of it. Most student teams are wary of evaluation and apprehensive about the process. They need to learn that assessment will continue to be part of their working world from now on. They should never be surprised at the results of an external evaluation—and they will not be if they self-assess regularly. These lessons are not lost on the students when they go through this procedure.

The final question is really one that can be dealt with only after the students begin to work and to assess their work. It is useful at the outset to let the teams know that they should meet once in a while just to discuss how things are going and whether they have heard of any new information or techniques that would allow them to work more efficiently. Thus, it is built into the team's work process from the very start that the members should be constantly on the alert for new or different ways to work. This activity teaches team members to scan their environments as part of their everyday work practice. If a member does bring up a new way to work, then the team needs to agree at the outset on how to handle the idea. The most effective way is to have a decision-making meeting during which the alternatives will be systematically evaluated.

This decision-making intervention is a useful procedure to ensure that team members are all working from the same set of assumptions, adhering to the same set of rules, and able to cope with diverse perspectives in a nonthreatening way. These techniques are particularly useful in project teams that need to produce results quickly. However, they are also valuable for the more traditional standing teams.

Successful Work Processes

Teams need to get down to work and begin producing their outputs. That is the purpose for which they were created. However, although team members may be very busy, they may not be spending their time on the most appropriate tasks or they may be accomplishing them inefficiently. Therefore, it is very important to scrutinize the current work processes of the team to ensure that the most effective processes are being used. The reason to do so is that effective work processes lead directly to successful team outputs.

CHAPTER EIGHT

HOLDING EFFECTIVE MEETINGS, MAKING DECISIONS, AND MANAGING CONFLICT

Teams seem to have particular difficulty with three processes: holding effective team meetings, making team decisions, and managing conflict. It has been my experience that teams generally find meetings frustrating and a waste of time. In addition, conflicting opinions over what decision to make can escalate into team dysfunction. Conflict between team members can make the team stall in accomplishing its work. All three of these issues come up all too frequently for most teams. Therefore the focus of this chapter is to make these team issues "non-issues," as much as is possible.

Holding Team Meetings

Meetings, and the time they take away from "on-task" work, are among the primary reasons why individual employees do not actively espouse working on teams. Whereas individuals can work on their own at their own pace, teams often need to meet face-to-face to get their work done. Because time is one of the most valued resources in organizational life these days (see Chapter Two), team members always appreciate it when meetings are conducted effectively and efficiently.

A number of technical advances can assist teams in meeting without having to get together in person. *Groupware*, as it is called, will be addressed in some detail in Chapter Eleven. The subject of this chapter is face-to-face team meetings.

There are a number of references on how to conduct effective meetings (for example, Auger, 1972; Carnes, 1980; Tropman, 1996; Tropman & Morningstar, 1985). However, even before calling a meeting and using these sources, teams often have questions, such as, Why should meetings be called? How often should they be called? Who should call them? Who should attend? How long should they be? When teams answer these questions, it provides a meeting framework. Although some of the answers seem obvious to those who have called, attended, and run many meetings, it is not surprising that many teams have trouble with these issues; most people do not have the experience of calling and running meetings. It is not an inborn skill. Teams that are expected to run themselves are often put in the odd position of conducting a meeting with no clue about how to do so.

Types of Meetings to Call

Face-to-face meetings with all team members present should be called for one or more of four reasons: *disseminating specific information, making decisions, sharing general information,* and *celebrating successes or other events.* If there is no reason to have a meeting, then one should not be called.

Each of these meeting types requires a slightly different technique. However, each one must be called and each one requires an agenda.

Specific Information Meetings. The first reason to call a team meeting is when specific information relevant to the entire team's goals needs to be disseminated and its ramifications for work discussed. This new information may call for a change in work process or structure, so all team members need to know it. If the information affects only a portion of the team, then only those members affected need to be called to the meeting. The others can be informed via memo or e-mail.

For example, if a team is working on a six-month project and the client wants the product or report a month earlier than expected, then the team needs to meet to discuss how to accommodate this new scheduling. It may mean that other projects will be put on hold for the time being, or that team members will be expected to work overtime, or that outside short-term help will have to be hired. Clearly this information will affect all team members, and action must be taken to deal with it.

Another example is if a team is planning its marketing strategy and a new technology becomes available to assist in the exercise (such as the Internet and World Wide Web). A marketing team meeting on this is necessary, and the sooner the better.

Whereas it is desirable in general to schedule a meeting well in advance to accommodate various members' schedules, the imperative nature of the specific information meeting requires a short lead time. The team leader should call the meeting and arrange a location appropriate for the type of information to be presented.

Although some meetings have lengthy agendas, specific information meetings should usually have only one agenda item: the information itself and its impact on work. If possible, the information and an assessment of its potential impact on the team's work should be provided to members in advance so that they come prepared to discuss the issue. The documentation circulated should not be alarmist in tone; rather, it should indicate what the new information entails, emphasize that the information to be discussed is important, and ask members to bring ideas about how to cope with the information.

Decision-Making Meetings. The second instance when team members need to get together is when a decision needs to be made that affects the entire team's work. It is important that the decision-making meeting be conducted in a systematic manner so that a team decision is actually rendered and all members understand and are comfortable with the decision. Even if all members do not fully agree with the decision, all of them should be able to describe the decision process as having been fair and the final decision as being informed. As with the first type of meeting, if a decision affects only part of the team then only those members need to meet. The outcome and rationale for the decision need to be provided to the rest of the team for informational purposes.

A decision-making meeting should be called by the leader well in advance. Information about the decision to be made must be circulated well before the meeting if it is to effective. Information surrounding the decision should include any background information, proposals, or other information pertinent to the decision. If this information is not circulated ahead of time, valuable meeting time is wasted as members try to do the reading. In contrast, if the information is circulated before the meeting, members have ample opportunity to think about the decision to be made, viable alternatives, and the pros and cons of each of the alternatives. Indeed, the team members should be assigned to do this kind of thinking as homework; they should come to the meeting prepared to discuss alternatives.

General Information Meetings. The third instance when teams need to get together is for general information exchange and updates. Particularly if the team is large, if the task is complex, or if a project takes place over an extended period of time, the team should get together at regular intervals. These meetings are needed to keep the team feeling like a team, rather than a collection of subteams or individual workers.

These meetings often can be—and should be—scheduled well in advance. If regular meetings are scheduled in advance, team members can leave the time open. For example, a team may decide it needs to meet once every two weeks for an hour on Tuesday mornings a 9:00 A.M. Another team may consider it more efficient to meet once a month for two or three hours. The number of meetings and their length is entirely determined by how frequently all team members need to be apprised of other members' activities.

The location of the meeting should remain the same from one meeting to the next. This consistency of time and place gives a sense of continuity to the team and its work.

The agenda for the meeting should include all general business and reports from members or subteams responsible for various aspects of the team's work. A set amount of time is designated for each member to describe his or her work, and the chair of the meeting must ensure that the agenda and time frames are adhered to as closely as possible. If any agenda items require background, that information should be circulated ahead of time so that members will not be reading when they need to be listening.

Informational meetings are the ones most likely to be poorly attended if they are not conducted efficiently. This is not the time for members to socialize. It is a time for information exchange. If these meetings are conducted well, the whole team will be induced to attend.

This type of meeting builds confidence among team members that they are progressing toward the goals. It is surprising how much work a team can accomplish, and when all the members get together to share their collective progress, it boosts the team's efficacy.

Celebratory Meetings. The fourth instance when teams need to meet is for celebration purposes. Celebrations may be held seasonally, in honor of individual and team successes, to thank individuals for their assistance, to welcome new members, and the like. Although no work per se gets done at these meetings, they are critical for team members to feel a sense of cohesion.

Team leaders can delegate the calling and organizing of these meetings to various members. It is best to schedule the meetings during regular working hours so that all members can attend. These meetings need to be called well in advance because often a large number of schedules have to be coordinated. Invitations may be more appropriate than agendas. Certainly if individuals external to the team are asked to attend, then invitations are necessary.

There may be some formal presentation at the meeting (a member may receive a plaque, or the company president may offer the team a congratulations, for example), but after a short ceremony the atmosphere at these meetings is a relaxed one that fosters socializing.

These meetings are easy for teams to overlook because they seem to be off-task. They are sometimes difficult to schedule and may seem to be "fluff." This may be true. If a team works together for only a short time on a simple project, then a celebration may not be in order. However, teams that are together for the long haul—whether crews, task forces, or standing teams—should have the opportunity to actively celebrate their team.

Rarely do teams have the luxury of sitting back and thinking about what they have done, who has helped them along the way, or how a new member or retiring member feels. Time should be set aside for such things, because they are what make the team unique. Without moments like these, the work environment can become very stale for team members.

Evaluating Meetings

Running an effective meeting is not a natural skill for most people. Rather, it is a skill that can be developed, and teams can develop it as well. Just as teams actively evaluate all aspects of their work, they should also actively evaluate their meeting work. Exhibit 8.1 presents a checklist of evaluation criteria for meeting effectiveness.

One of the best ways to help team meetings become more effective over the long term is to debrief about the meeting itself. This debriefing takes the form of a meeting critique, carried out by all team members, using the criteria noted in Exhibit 8.1. However, the conduct of team members is also important. In particular, how well the meeting was chaired, how the agenda was handled, and how members conducted themselves should be evaluated. Suggestions for items like these include those noted in Exhibit 8.2. The list is not meant to be all-inclusive but rather to start team members thinking about how they want their meetings to be conducted.

Conclusions About Meetings

Teams now have, if they did not before, a framework for team meetings. I did not delve into issues surrounding running the meetings themselves. As noted earlier, there are several very useful references written just about this task.

The evaluation process may take the team some time at first, but after engaging in it a couple of times, teams that have had difficulty accomplishing their work in meetings will soon find that their meetings are actually effective and worth attending!

EXHIBIT 8.1. CRITERIA FOR AN EFFECTIVE MEETING

These criteria should be adhered to as closely as possible for all team meetings. Teams can use this as a checklist to determine where they can improve the effectiveness and efficiency of their meetings.

1. Agenda created so that the meeting is deemed necessary and important for members to attend
2. Agenda circulated well enough in advance of the meeting so that members have time to prepare for the meeting
3. Supporting documentation or materials relevant to the meeting circulated so that members had time to read, digest, and think about the issues to be brought up at the meeting
4. Time (start *and* stop) and location of meeting clearly stated on the agenda and room for meeting booked
5. Materials needed for the meeting (for example, flip charts, overhead projector, slide projector, and so on) booked and ready for the meeting
6. Meeting started on time
7. Members prepared to discuss agenda items
8. Agenda worked through to completion
9. Notes taken on issues that need to be recorded
10. Action items assigned to individual members
11. Remaining or unresolved issues to be brought forward to next meeting
12. Closure reached on as many agenda items as possible
13. Meeting ended on time
14. Sense of accomplishment and time spent well by meeting participants
15. Action items and/or minutes of the meeting distributed to members as soon as possible following the meeting so that members are clear on what they are to do for the next meeting

Making Team Decisions

One of the most common agenda items at meetings regards making a team decision. Sometimes decision-making meetings can be long, drawn out, and unsystematic. This section describes a decision-making strategy that was designed to help groups make decisions in a systematic, unbiased manner: Multiple-Attribute Utility Analysis (MAU). This highly regarded approach has been used and evaluated in a number of decision contexts (for example, Einhorn & McCoach, 1977; Fischer, 1976; Huber, 1980; Keeney & Raiffa, 1976).

Multiple-Attribute Utility Analysis

The purpose of MAU is to examine critically a number of alternatives with the goal of arriving at a mutually agreed-upon team decision. MAU processes are context-dependent; that is, each context will provide different issues for the team

EXHIBIT 8.2. ASSESSMENT OF MEETING PROCESS.

All statements are first rated by each team member. Read each item and determine the extent to which the team agrees with the statement. This exercise should not be punitive—rather, be very constructive in responding to the items. Be prepared to say why you rated the items as you did. Have one member of the team place the average rating of all team members on another rating form. Discuss the items that are rated as a 1 or a 2 within the framework of making effective meetings a goal for the team.

	Completely disagree	Disagree somewhat	Neither agree nor disagree	Agree somewhat	Completely agree
Chair Issues					
1. The chair moved through the agenda.	1	2	3	4	5
2. The chair was impartial.	1	2	3	4	5
3. The chair asked all members for input.	1	2	3	4	5
Agenda Issues					
1. The agenda order was appropriate.	1	2	3	4	5
2. The agenda items were dealt with to the satisfaction of members.	1	2	3	4	5
3. The number of items on the agenda was appropriate.	1	2	3	4	5
Member Conduct Issues					
1. Team members were polite to one another.	1	2	3	4	5
2. Team members were constructively critical of any ideas discussed.	1	2	3	4	5
3. Team members came prepared to discuss the issues.	1	2	3	4	5

to work with. The steps of the MAU process, however, remain the same. In this section, the eight-step MAU process is described. Then, to make the steps more concrete, a case study example is presented.

A note of caution: the MAU process takes time. It is an inappropriate strategy in cases where time is of the essence (for example, a surgical team in the operating theater). This does not imply that crews should omit the procedure altogether; however, when the team must focus on the task at hand engaging in an MAU is contraindicated.

Step One: Identifying the Team's Purpose. The team members come to a consensus about what is important. If they are a task force, the team's purpose may have been provided in advance (for example, come up with a new safety program for the organization). Alternatively, the team may spend some time discussing what it wants to achieve in the long term (for example, a profitable company, a successful fundraising campaign, a well-recognized educational program, better job satisfaction among employees). In other words, this part of the process is at the very heart of why the team exists in the first place. These issues should have been resolved during the goal-setting stages discussed in Chapter Four; if they remain unresolved, then that becomes apparent during the MAU process.

Step Two: Generating Alternatives. Assuming that a common perception of why the team exists is clear and shared by all team members, the next step is to generate all possible alternatives regarding a particular decision. The number of alternatives may be relatively straightforward, such as when a yes-or-no decision must be made (for example, hire a new person or not, branch out into a new market or not, proceed with a tax increase or not). However, when there are many possibilities, generating alternatives can be a very complicated process. For example, if an organization must become more cost-effective then the team may come up with several alternatives, such as downsize across the board, close particular units, increase team-based work, or shift employees into new parts of the business.

Step Three: Listing Consequences. Next, the team lists each of the consequences associated with each alternative. The list of consequences will be the *same* for each alternative. For example, if an organization is deciding whether to move into a new market, the consequences of a yes or a no decision will be the same, likely including staffing issues, financial issues, distribution issues, and others.

Step Four: Rating Consequence Importance. The team then rates the importance (on a scale of 0 to 10) of each consequence. Here is where team members' differences of opinion (if there are any) about why the team exists will surface. For example, if a consequence of downsizing is assumed to be an effect on employee morale, and I view that as important, I may want to rate the consequence as a 10. If one of my other team members views the consequence of affected employee morale as less important, he may want to rate it as a 5. There is usually a lot of discussion among team members at this step, and dissenting philosophies may need to be worked through in the course of attaching the importance ratings to the consequences.

If the team members have highly similar perceptions, then they may be able to work through the MAU process themselves. If it is known beforehand that the members have fundamentally different perceptions about what is important, then the MAU should be facilitated by an outsider who can take on the role of chair, facilitator, or even referee if needed.

Step Five: Rating the Utility of the Consequences. The next step is for the team to rate the utility of each importance rating for each alternative. These utility ratings are the negative or positive impact that the consequence for a particular alternative will have on the team's purpose. These values usually range from -100 to $+100$, but some teams prefer to use a scale of -10 to $+10$, or even -5 to $+5$, to make the final computations easier. For example, consider again a team that is examining downsizing across the board versus closing particular units; one of the consequences will be affected employee morale. If across-the-board cuts are chosen, then employee morale may be seen to be affected at a level of -75 because all units will be affected. If unit closures are chosen, then employee morale may be seen to be affected at a level of -25 because only some units will be affected.

Step Six: Generating Total Scores. The sixth step is to generate total scores for each alternative by cross-multiplying the importance ratings by the utility ratings and then summing the resulting values for each alternative. Total scores for each alternative may be positive or negative. The total scores are determined by two factors: how important the consequence is and how great an impact the consequence will have for the alternative in question. Total scores will increase substantially as consequences deemed important are perceived to be positively affected by a given alternative (because of the multiplication). Conversely, total scores will decrease substantially as consequences deemed important are perceived to be negatively affected by the alternative.

Step Seven: Ranking Alternatives. In the seventh step, the team rank-orders the alternatives on the basis of total scores (from most positive to most negative). The ranking should give the team a rationally based idea of the most suitable alternative for the decision at hand.

Step Eight: Discussing Outcomes. At the eighth step, the team members discuss the degree to which the final ranking reflects their own gut feelings about the decision. That is, there needs to be an assessment of the extent to which the hard numbers of the total scores are reflective of the group's own feelings about the issue. If the numerical and gut-feel assessments seem to be congruent, then the MAU process ends. If the ranking seems to be counterintuitive, the team members go back through the consequences, importance ratings, and utility rating steps to see *why* the alternatives were scored as they were. This review helps the team determine why the final ranking occurred, and it is a key benefit of the MAU process.

Benefits of the MAU Process

The MAU process is an iterative one. At any time, changes can be made to the list of consequences, importance ratings, or utility ratings. Once a total score for each alternative model is generated, the total scores are examined and compared. The intent is not to accept blindly the alternative with the highest total score as necessarily the preferred alternative.

There is no accepted metric for deciding how high a total score has to be or how far apart total scores between alternatives must be before a preferred alternative can be considered the obvious one. Rather, the purpose of the total scores is to engage the team in a discussion of how the total scores were arrived at in the first place. For example, one alternative may have had a highly negative utility rating on a consequence deemed to be important, thus greatly lowering the total score for that alternative. It is useful for the team to go back and explore whether the consequence is indeed that important or whether that negative utility should have been so high.

By its very nature, the MAU promotes a discussion of whether the group is in agreement with the accepted alternative based on the total score. Any discomfort with the solution in question is examined by reviewing the consequence list for errors of omission or errors of commission, and reviewing both the importance ratings and the utility ratings.

The goal of the MAU analysis is to make decision making explicit and transparent. It forces team members to consider which consequences they consider important and what the implications are for each alternative model for these consequences. When an alternative is finally chosen, it is because the decision makers have carefully considered all of the possible alternatives, thought through all of the various consequences that will result from any alternative, weighed the relative importance of each of these consequences in light of the team's purpose, examined the impact (utility) of each alternative on each consequence, and taken the time systematically to reexamine the decision that was reached, particularly if it is not congruent with team members' expectations.

The MAU does not merely help teams select the alternative that best fits their goals and objectives. The procedure also makes decision making systematic, explicit, and procedurally fair to team members. It forces team members to articulate what they care about in the organization and why. The process reminds the participants of this information as they work through the various alternatives. It helps to organize, in a systematic way, large amounts of information that should be taken into account when making important decisions. In addition, it makes reporting the decision to outsiders easy—in that the rationale for the decision is obvious upon examination of the consequences, importance ratings, and utility values.

The following case study demonstrates how to use a Multiple-Attribute Utility Analysis effectively.

Case Study: A Multiple-Attribute Utility Analysis

Organization X is interested in reorganizing the work its staff carries out. Currently, individuals work primarily on their own, in functional and hierarchically defined units. This organization is a well-known accounting firm that employs approximately five hundred people. There is no financial imperative to restructure: the organization is not suffering from low profits or threat of closing. Instead, the president feels that the organization can be more productive. A task force is established to identify ways to change the organization structure or work processes to increase productivity. An MAU process is invoked and the following outcomes result:

Step One: Purpose of the Team

Increase productivity.

Step Two: Generate Alternatives

1. Leave things as they are as a point of comparison to any alternatives.
2. Create teams within functional units.
3. Create teams across functional units.
4. Decrease the workforce by firing nonproductive people.
5. Create an employee profit-sharing plan as an incentive to be more productive.

Step Three: List Consequences

A. Individual employee job satisfaction

B. Long-term financial costs

C. Short-term disruption in work procedures

D. Building a team organization

E. Increasing work throughput

F. Resources needed to implement change

G. Customer satisfaction

H. Long-term profitability

Step Four: Rate Consequence Importance (from 0 to 10)

A. Individual employee job satisfaction	2
B. Long-term financial costs	4
C. Short-term disruption in work procedures	1
D. Building a team organization	6
E. Increasing work throughput	9
F. Resources needed to implement change	5
G. Customer satisfaction	6
H. Long-term profitability	10

Step Five: Rate Utilities (from –100 to +100)

Alternative 1. Leave things as they are as a point of comparison to any alternatives. (Note that because there is no change in this alternative, the impact for each consequence is 0.)

A. Individual employee job satisfaction	0
B. Long-term financial costs	0
C. Short-term disruption in work procedures	0
D. Building a team organization	0
E. Increasing work throughput	0
F. Resources needed to implement change	0
G. Customer satisfaction	0
H. Long-term profitability	0

Alternative 2. Create teams within functional units.

A. Individual employee job satisfaction	+10
B. Long-term financial costs	+10
C. Short-term disruption in work procedures	–60
D. Building a team organization	+50

E. Increasing work throughput	+15
F. Resources needed to implement change	−50
G. Customer satisfaction	0
H. Long-term profitability	+15

Alternative 3. Create teams across functional units.

A. Individual employee job satisfaction	+10
B. Long-term financial costs	+20
C. Short-term disruption in work procedures	−75
D. Building a "team" organization	+60
E. Increasing work throughput	+20
F. Resources needed to implement change	−70
G. Customer satisfaction	+5
H. Long-term profitability	+20

Alternative 4. Decrease the workforce by firing nonproductive people.

A. Individual employee job satisfaction	−50
B. Long-term financial costs	+10
C. Short-term disruption in work procedures	−40
D. Building a "team" organization	−20
E. Increasing work throughput	+15
F. Resources needed to implement change	−40
G. Customer satisfaction	0
H. Long-term profitability	+10

Alternative 5. Create an employee profit-sharing plan as an incentive to be more productive.

A. Individual employee job satisfaction	+25
B. Long-term financial costs	−10
C. Short-term disruption in work procedures	−15
D. Building a "team" organization	0
E. Increasing work throughput	+25
F. Resources needed to implement change	−25
G. Customer satisfaction	+15
H. Long-term profitability	+30

Step Six: Generate Total Scores

Alternative 1. Leave things as they are as a point of comparison to any alternatives.

A. Individual employee job satisfaction	$0 \times 2 = 0$
B. Long-term financial costs	$0 \times 4 = 0$
C. Short-term disruption in work procedures	$0 \times 1 = 0$
D. Building a team organization	$0 \times 6 = 0$
E. Increasing work throughput	$0 \times 9 = 0$
F. Resources needed to implement change	$0 \times 5 = 0$
G. Customer satisfaction	$0 \times 6 = 0$
H. Long-term profitability	$0 \times 10 = 0$
	Total score = 0

Alternative 2. Create teams within functional units.

A. Individual employee job satisfaction	$+10 \times 2 = +20$
B. Long-term financial costs	$+10 \times 4 = +40$
C. Short-term disruption in work procedures	$-60 \times 1 = -60$
D. Building a team organization	$+50 \times 6 = +300$
E. Increasing work throughput	$+15 \times 9 = +135$
F. Resources needed to implement change	$-50 \times 5 = -250$
G. Customer satisfaction	$0 \times 6 = 0$
H. Long-term profitability	$+15 \times 10 = +150$
	Total score = +335

Alternative 3. Create teams across functional units.

A. Individual employee job satisfaction	$+10 \times 2 = +20$
B. Long-term financial costs	$+20 \times 4 = +80$
C. Short-term disruption in work procedures	$-75 \times 1 = -75$
D. Building a team organization	$+60 \times 6 = +360$
E. Increasing work throughput	$+20 \times 9 = +180$
F. Resources needed to implement change	$-70 \times 5 = -350$
G. Customer satisfaction	$+5 \times 6 = +30$
H. Long-term profitability	$+20 \times 10 = +200$
	Total score = +445

Alternative 4. Decrease the workforce by firing nonproductive people.

A. Individual employee job satisfaction	$-50 \times 2 = -100$
B. Long-term financial costs	$+10 \times 4 = +40$
C. Short-term disruption in work procedures	$-40 \times 1 = -40$
D. Building a team organization	$-20 \times 6 = +120$
E. Increasing work throughput	$+15 \times 9 = +135$
F. Resources needed to implement change	$-40 \times 5 = -200$
G. Customer satisfaction	$0 \times 6 = 0$
H. Long-term profitability	$+10 \times 10 = +100$
	Total score = +55

Alternative 5. Create an employee profit-sharing plan as an incentive to be more productive.

A. Individual employee job satisfaction	$+25 \times 2 = +50$
B. Long-term financial costs	$-10 \times 4 = -40$
C. Short-term disruption in work procedures	$-15 \times 1 = -15$
D. Building a team organization	$0 \times 6 = 0$
E. Increasing work throughput	$+25 \times 9 = +225$
F. Resources needed to implement change	$-25 \times 5 = -125$
G. Customer satisfaction	$+15 \times 6 = +90$
H. Long-term profitability	$+30 \times 10 = +300$
	Total score = +485

Step Seven: Rank Alternatives Based on Total Scores

1. Alternative 5. Create an employee profit-sharing plan as an incentive to be more productive: Total score = +485.
2. Alternative 3. Create teams across functional units: Total score = +445
3. Alternative 2. Create teams within functional units: Total score = +335.
4. Alternative 4. Decrease the workforce by firing nonproductive people: Total score = +55
5. Alternative 1. Leave things as they are as a benchmark: Total score = 0

Step Eight: Discuss Outcomes of the MAU

The results of this particular MAU are definitely worth discussing. First, the task force notes that the least desirable alternative is to leave things as they are. According to the MAU, any one of the four other alternatives will show an improvement on the consequences deemed important to the organization.

The second thing the task force notes is that Alternatives 3 and 5 are close in value (+445 and +485, respectively) although they represent completely different ways to go about changing the organization. The task force decides to examine the scores in greater detail.

First, Alternative 3 receives a positive boost from the "building a team" consequence. This makes perfect sense, in that building teams could be expected to increase the team consequence. However, there is a large negative value associated with the resources needed to implement the change. There is also a very low utility value (–70) associated with the short-term disruption consequence, but the task force had deemed the importance of this consequence to be 1 and so it translates into only –70 in the calculation of Alternative 3's total score.

Turning to Alternative 5, the task force sees that it receives its most positive points from the consequences of increasing work throughput and long-term profitability, whereas the consequence of building a team organization is rated as 0. The task force notes that the utility value associated with short-term disruption consequence for this alternative is small (–15) in comparison with that of Alternative 3.

In comparing Alternatives 3 and 5, the task force discusses the fact that the personnel in the organization are very traditional and conservative. Therefore, although Alternatives 3 and 5 were close in their final scores, the team deems Alternative 5 to be more palatable and easier to implement in this particular organization.

In addition to revisiting Alternatives 3 and 5 in detail, the task force also examines Alternatives 2 and 4. The task force members decide that if they choose a team solution, the organization might as well go all the way and create cross-functional teams. They therefore agree that Alternative 2 (creating teams within functional units) would be highly disruptive yet would not provide the higher level of long-term profitability that the cross-functional teams would be expected to provide.

Alternative 4 (laying off workers) is deemed personally unacceptable to the task force members. They feel that the organization's employees are generally hardworking and that the low morale that is a consequence of a layoff situation would make this approach inappropriate, especially because the organization is not suffering financially.

The task force goes back through the list of consequences to determine if in the course of its discussions other potential consequences were missed or some of the consequences should have been omitted. The members decide that this is not the case. (If it were, then they would need to change the list of consequences for each alternative, provide importance ratings for them, provide utility ratings for them, and then recalculate the total scores.)

Next, the task force goes back and determines if the importance ratings given to each consequence are still reasonable to all members; they agree that the importance ratings are fine. (Again, if they had decided to change the importance ratings, they would need to recalculate total scores for each alternative and revisit the final ranking of alternatives.)

Finally, the task force goes back over each utility rating for each alternative and determines if the members still agree on these ratings. The task force does. However, if it did not, it would need to recalculate the total scores for the alternatives in which the changes were made to see if there was a resultant change in the ranking of alternatives.

At the end of the MAU procedure, the task force decides that Alternative 5 is the one to be recommended to the president. When the task force recommends it, it will be able to tell the president—and the rest of the organization—exactly why this particular alternative was the most attractive. The members can be confident that they examined the alternatives systematically, gave fair and equitable time to each alternative as they thought each one through (that is, no alternative was dismissed out of hand), and arrived at a consensual decision. Given the political nature of organizations, these benefits of the MAU process are as important as having come up with the best alternative in the first place.

Now if circumstances change, or if the president comes up with another alternative that the task force must examine, or if the organization's personnel changes substantially over the next six months, then the MAU can be conducted again using the same process. The members of the task force may then be ready to carry the MAU out on their own, whereas for the first MAU, they may have needed some assistance to ensure that the process moved along in a timely manner and was conducted appropriately.

This case shows how a typical MAU works. It is an excellent vehicle for team decision making when there is sufficient time for exploration of alternatives. It is particularly useful, then, in a politically charged environment. It is also very useful when a team is just starting out and needs to determine its priorities. Most of the decisions a team needs to make could utilize the MAU process, although its time-consuming nature would suggest that it may best be reserved for major decisions.

Managing Conflict

One of the most effective ways to ensure team failure is to allow conflict among team members to get out of hand. Fortunately, because most teamwork occurs in the work environment, much team conflict is not personal in nature. Despite the claims from some team members that their team is dysfunctional because of "personality conflicts," rarely is this the case. Instead, team conflict most frequently stems from different work priorities or different work values.

When dealing with team conflict, it is most important to keep the focus of the conflict on the work and the task—not on any individual. In this section, then, I assume that conflicts are most often rooted in differences between members with strongly held beliefs or dissimilar performance norms. There are several highly effective steps that the team can take when it becomes mired in conflict to get it working smoothly again. It should be noted that, if team members are experiencing conflict but are still able to work with each other, the team may be able to work through the conflict on its own. However, if the team members are not even on speaking terms, they will need the services of an outside facilitator to work through the conflict management process.

First, the team members need to ensure that they agree on the purpose of the team. For a surgical crew, the purpose may be to successfully carry out an open-heart surgery in the most effective way possible. For a landscape design team, it may be to design a school landscape in the most pleasing and affordable manner possible. All team members need to recognize that they do, in fact, have a common goal. If the members do not agree on the common goal, then the team really should be dissolved or helped to identify its purpose to the satisfaction of all members.

Recognizing a common purpose is often *not* the problem in conflict management. In fact, once the members step back from their positions of conflict and agree that they agree on the overall reason for the team's existence, much of the battle has been won. It is heartening to realize that the team member with whom you were having a conflict really wants the same things as you do in the long run. This helps change the focus of the conflict from having different opinions to solving the issue at hand.

Second, the team identifies all its areas of agreement. For example, the team should review its goals, subgoals, goal completion times, performance norms, and other issues specific to the team. Using a flip chart or whiteboard, the issues that the team agrees on are put down in one area. The issues around which there is disparity are put down in another area. Team members who entered the session in great conflict are often surprised to find that they actually agree on a large number of issues.

Third, the team determines if the differences noted are actually interfering with the team's work. If they are not, then members simply agree to disagree. Only issues that will make the team's work suffer deserve the team's attention. Decide which of the issues is most problematic for the team as a whole. Then go about discussing alternative ways of working (perhaps using an MAU process) so that these points of contention are dealt with. Teams should be cautioned not to try to resolve all differences at once; doing so is overwhelming. Instead, the team needs to resolve the most pressing points of disagreement first. Many of the other issues may disappear as the team begins to work together, accomplish its goals, and feel successful.

Fourth, if it is necessary, team members can bring up concerns about other team members. This must be done with care. Before holding such a meeting, all members must agree to a set of protocols. For example, a good protocol to adopt is to listen to other team members. This includes allowing each member to finish speaking and then paraphrasing what that person said. Even if all members don't agree with the statement, the speaker will appreciate that the rest of the team understands what he or she is trying to convey. Assign one person to record the major points of concern brought up by members so that the points are not forgotten. What this process does is slow down escalating conflict situations.

Another protocol to observe is for the person who responds to a speaker to build on that speaker's statement. This assists in moving the conversation forward, and yet keeps it from becoming disjointed. Another protocol members need to agree to is to bring up a specific concern about any member only once. A final protocol members should adhere to is to try to remain calm during the discussions. This may be hard to do, and when the situation seems to be becoming emotionally charged something needs to be done to calm it down again. Ways to keep the situation in hand include taking a break and leaving the room to "cool off" (going for a coffee break or lunch, perhaps), using humor to put some perspective on the situation, saying "I'm sorry" and "Thank you" to other members as needed, showing respect for others, and not using profane language. Team Exercise 8.3 summarizes the steps in managing conflict.

To resolve individual concerns, the approach to use is similar to that used to resolve task-oriented disagreements. That is, first decide if any concerns interfere with the team's work. If there are some concerns, then determine which one or ones must be resolved so that the team can function. Then, the team discusses alternative ways to resolve the concerns. Finally, team members agree to uphold any commitments they made during the session.

One of the important things to note is that there will be conflict in teams no matter how well the members like each other. Much of the conflict is irrelevant and shouldn't be made much of or it will slow the team down. Destructive conflict is that which keeps the team from functioning at its highest level or leaves one or more members disheartened about participating on the team. If this occurs, then going through the outlined steps should help the team manage its conflicts.

Successful Meetings, Successful Decision Making, and Managed Conflict

Three of the more anxiety-provoking activities for teams are holding meetings, making decisions, and managing conflict. The exercises provided in this chapter will assist teams in having more effective meetings, ensuring that decisions are made fairly and effectively, and managing conflicts successfully. If teams hold effective meetings, make effective decisions, and are not sidetracked by team conflict, they will be well on their way to effective performance.

CHAPTER NINE

EVALUATING TEAM OUTCOMES

One of the most common complaints of team members is that they do not receive enough performance feedback. This is surprising for two reasons. First, teams are often created to enhance the productivity of an organization, so it seems strange indeed that there is a lack of mechanisms to evaluate their effectiveness. Second, the commonly accepted notion is that employees do not like performance evaluations, so team members' desire for feedback is contradictory. However, even though it may be surprising, it is clearly true that an explicit, detailed, and fair evaluation system for teams needs to be in place in order for teams to perform well, both for organizational effectiveness and for performance management purposes.

In a study on team evaluation, one of the findings was that—if they were evaluated at all—teams were evaluated as individual workers, not as teams (Kline & McGrath, 1998). This finding was consistent with the fact that most performance management systems use individual performance as the metric for a number of important decisions, including pay raises, promotion decisions, and training need determinations.

For an organization to change these individually based procedures into team-based procedures, virtually the entire system must be overhauled. As a result, organizations have been slow to tackle the problem of team performance. The academic community has also been slow to provide organizations with any guidance in team assessment. Some of the most recent research (Welbourne, Johnson, & Erez, 1998) that touts the importance of the team role evaluates that particular role at the individual level. Only recently have any books or articles provided ideas on how to go about evaluating teams (for example, Brannick, Salas, & Prince, 1997; Kline & McGrath, 1998).

Defining Effectiveness

Several authors have put forward ideas about what it means for a team to be effective. One common thread is that the evaluation of teams needs to be made on different levels. Specifically, hard measures of team performance are necessary, such as quality of work and quantity of work output. In addition, softer variables are critical, such as how well the team members get along and how well member needs are satisfied.

For example, in their work with anti–air warfare teams on navy ships, Dickinson and McIntyre (1997) suggest seven factors to be evaluated when measuring teams for effectiveness: team orientation, team leadership, communication, monitoring, feedback, backup behavior, and coordination. Kraiger and Wenzel (1997) distinguish between evaluating team effectiveness as tangible outcomes (for example, product quality, costs, time, errors, productivity) and evaluating team effectiveness as work processes (for example, communication, assertiveness, morale, leadership). Sundstrom, DeMeuse, and Futrell (1990) state that there is a difference between outputs of the team as one dimension of performance and team viability as a separate dimension of effectiveness. In his model of team effectiveness, Hackman (1987) posits three dimensions to group effectiveness: acceptability of task output, capability of the members to work together in the future, and the satisfaction of team members as individuals.

Assessing teams on different dimensions of performance is consistent with the differentiation that occurs in the literature on the evaluation of individual performance. Here, assessments of the effort put in on the job (process) versus the outputs of the job (outcomes) are treated as separate aspects of performance. The remainder of this chapter will be devoted to what might be typically referred to as the outcomes side of evaluation. However, these outcomes are not just outputs of the team—they are observable aspects of team performance. That is, outsiders as well as team members themselves can make judgments about the team's outcome effectiveness. Chapter Ten will discuss the internal, process aspects of team effectiveness—those that can best be judged by the team members themselves.

Evaluating Observables

The two-part study by Kline and McGrath (1998) is unique in that in the first part we asked twenty-six team members, team facilitators, and team supervisors which dimensions of performance they wanted to use as part of a team evaluation process. In the second part, twenty-five team members, team supervisors, and team facilitators (none of whom participated in the first part) validated the findings from the first sample. These participants worked in actual teams across several different organizations and thus the results are based on actual teamwork experience.

We found five primary dimensions of team performance, each made up of a number of different components. They are described in Exhibit 9.1.

The virtues of this particular five-dimension approach are several. First, the items and dimensions have been created by teams themselves. No preconceived notion of team performance was imposed on the participants. Therefore, they were free to identify what they deemed important. Second, the participants did not just provide one perspective; team members, supervisors, and facilitators were fully involved in the process. Third, the five dimensions are broad enough to cut across almost all team lines—whether they are standing teams, task forces, or crews; whether they are in the private, public, or nonprofit sector; whether they are in different units within the same organization. Fourth, the specific components that make up each dimension are the ones we found in our particular study. Teams may decide that different components would be more appropriate for their team in their context. For example, a functional team with no budget per se may deem the staying-within-budget component to be irrelevant to the meeting objectives dimension.

Using the Evaluation

Several issues need to be resolved before a team should launch into using this (or any other) evaluation scheme. I will highlight the issues as they pertain to this particular evaluation tool.

Determining Components

The first task of the team is to determine the components for each dimension. The team members and supervisor need to walk through each dimension and think of the components relevant to it that pertain to that particular team. It is

EXHIBIT 9.1. DIMENSIONS OF TEAM PERFORMANCE.

1. Problem Solving

a. Determination of team goals and objectives
b. Alignment of the team's objectives with the organization's goals
c. Number of different alternatives suggested by the team in solving problems
d. Fairness and effectiveness of procedure used in determining the best alternative

2. Quality of Work

a. Care that has gone into the team's work
b. Number of errors committed
c. Amount of "backtracking" that needs to be done because the product/service was not done correctly the first time
d. Customer satisfaction

3. Workload Allocation

a. Equitable distribution of the team's workload
b. Effective use of each team member's skill set such that the best person for any one task is working on that task
c. Each team member's contributions of value to the end product/service

4. Meeting Objectives

a. Meeting goals and objectives
b. Staying within budget
c. Staying within time frame

5. Team Attitude

a. Cooperativeness of team members
b. Information sharing among team members
c. Commitment to team goals by team members
d. Respect for one another shown among team members

Source: Kline, T.J.B., & McGrath, J. "Development and Validation of Five Criteria for Evaluating Team Performance." *Organization Development Journal, 16,* 22, 1998. Adapted with permission.

helpful for the team to have at least three or more components associated with each dimension. By so doing, the team provides itself a degree of measurement reliability for the dimensions.

Assigning Anchor Points

Next, the anchoring points that will be used to evaluate the team on each component need to be determined. In our research program, we use a 5-point scale ranging from a low value of 1 to a high value of 5, where 3 indicates an average level of performance. In some organizations, a 3-point scale with anchors of "1 = does not meet expectations," "2 = meets expectations," and "3 = exceeds expectations" may suffice. In other organizations a 7-point rating scale may be more appropriate, with a low value of 1, a high value of 7, and 4 indicating average performance.

The anchoring system selected should be the one that will work best in the particular organization. For example, some organizations already use point scales for performance. If this is the case, then any new team rating scale should conform to typical practice. If the teams are just starting out and have a high degree of evaluation apprehension, then a 3-point scale may seem less offensive to the teams and, therefore, the evaluation process will be more likely to be used.

Determining Who Will Rate the Team

The next issue the team must come to agreement on is who will determine the performance ratings. In making this determination, one of the primary considerations is the extent to which the evaluator has access to the team and its outputs. Those who are going to rate the team's performance should be able to observe the team as it works, be a recipient of the outputs of the team, or both. Some evaluation forms provide a place to specify the amount of the rater's contact with the team. This information builds fairness into the process. If a certain customer has frequent contact with the team, then that person's perspective may carry more weight in the evaluation than the views of another customer who has had contact with the team only once.

One particular rater issue is that team and supervisor ratings of performance usually do not agree. Specifically, in our research this value was, on average, about 0.16 (where zero agreement is 0.00, a perfect positive agreement is 1.00, and a perfect negative agreement is −1.00). A reasonable agreement rate would be in the 0.80 range or better. Even *within* the team itself the agreement on ratings of performance is extremely low (0.25). Dealing with this inconsistency is the subject of the next section.

Using Frame-of-Reference Training

The best way to alleviate the problems of interrater inconsistency is through a performance rater training technique called Frame-of-Reference Training (FOR training, for short), developed by Bernardin and Buckley in 1981.

FOR training provides three distinct benefits. First, it gives raters a common perspective on performance. It has been highly successful in the evaluation of individual performance (for example, Sulsky & Day, 1992; Noonan, 1996), and the same should hold true in rating team performance.

Second, FOR training identifies the relevant dimensions of work performance. This issue was addressed earlier in this chapter, but recall that there is a high degree of latitude when it comes to the components that make up each dimension. Next, FOR training assists the raters in maintaining distinctions between what behaviors or components go with which performance dimension. For example, "meeting objectives within budget" belongs to the meeting objectives dimension and not the quality of work dimension. With FOR training, raters avoid contaminating aspects of one dimension with information that is supposed to be allocated to a different dimension.

Third, FOR gets all raters to agree on the performance levels associated with each rated component or dimension. That is, a 1 on the determination of goals and objectives component should mean the same thing to all team members and to the supervisor as well.

The FOR training format follows that of Pulakos (1984, 1989). In this format, definitions of each performance dimension are discussed. Next, the descriptions of each of the levels of performance are discussed. As many examples as possible are generated in these discussions, to enable the team members to understand what the performance dimensions are and what a particular level of performance means. In addition, there is detailed discussion about which behaviors or outcomes go with which dimension or component. Through these discussions, a common frame of reference for the particular team's performance in the particular organizational context is defined. All parties that are going to use the rating forms should be present at these discussions and be full participants. In the typical FOR training procedures, videotapes of either scripted or actual performance are shown; participants rate behavior and receive feedback on the accuracy of their ratings.

These procedures were developed for use in rating individual performance. The process can, and should, be used with teams. However, given the complex nature of teams and teamwork, the development of training materials will be time consuming.

Using the Evaluation Results

The final issue concerns what the evaluation will be used for, and it is by far the most politically sensitive and the one that causes the most problems in performance management. If the evaluation is to serve a developmental purpose (for example, feedback solely to the team for its own information and improvement), then the members are likely to be candid and constructive in their responses. If the evaluation is to be used to determine a pay raise, a promotion, a new office location, a new hire into the team, or some other personnel decision, then the procedure needs to be carried out in such a way as to be judged by the team as fair.

Procedural justice is an aspect of fairness that focuses on the process used to arrive at a decision, and this justice is high if the process is seen to be fair by all parties involved. For this reason, it is important that the process be documented and a paper trail of any decision made so that a rationale for decisions can be demonstrated to everyone's satisfaction. Clearly, this method will not alleviate all problems associated with decision outcomes that are unfavorable, but it will go a long way in stopping them from getting out of hand.

The following case study illustrates how a team can develop and use a team performance evaluation system based on the five dimensions.

Case Study: Creating a Team Evaluation

The government has requested that schools become more accountable for their funding. Each school board is assigned the task of creating a report and passes the assignment to the school level. Each school is required to come up with its own assessment of its accountability. The time frame for the task is nine months; the schools begin in September and the final report to the school board is due June 1.

The principal of Elementary School Y has asked a task force of three teachers, three parents, and two administrative personnel (not including the principal) to come up with a system to determine how well the school is carrying out its mission of educating local children. No budget is allocated to the task force, but expenses associated with collecting data and writing the report are covered. In addition, the school board has agreed to provide the services of a team coach to assist the task forces of the various schools.

The task force for School Y calls itself the Accountability Team (the A-Team). It has partially completed its assigned task, including preparing an interim report, and wants to evaluate itself on how well it is doing. The interim report and team evaluation will become part of School Y's annual report, which will go to the school board. To carry out its own evaluation, the A-Team gets together with the team coach to go through the process of creating a team evaluation idiosyncratic to the A-Team's purpose.

First, through discussion, the A-Team arrives at a list of components for each performance dimension. These are as follows:

Problem Solving

- School Y's multiple goals were determined early in the process, with the task force recognizing that many criteria could be used in evaluating the school's effectiveness (for example, intellectual skills, social skills, life skills, preparation for secondary school, accommodation of special needs students, job satisfaction of personnel, and so on).
- Procedures used to determine the priority of the different goals were fair.
- Procedures used to determine the priority of the different goals were effective.
- A number of different alternatives were suggested by the team in determining how to evaluate each of the multiple goals.

Quality of Work

- A large amount of person hours (time) went into the collection of the data associated with assessing how well School Y was able to accomplish each goal.
- Detailed information was collected to assess how well School Y was able to accomplish each goal.
- "Backtracking" that needed to be done because the correct information was not collected the first time was minimal.
- The interim report was well-organized and well-written, as determined by the principal and the president of the parent association of School Y.

Workload Allocation

- All members of the A-Team put in roughly the same number of hours on the task.
- Tasks were allocated to play to each member's strengths as much as possible.
- Each member had to do his or her fair share of "grunt work."

Meeting Objectives

- A detailed cost-accounting of all dollars spent to carry out the task to date was kept.
- The interim report contained the data that were expected.
- The interim report was completed with enough time allowed for review of the report by the principal and the president of the parent association of School Y so that revisions could be made before sending it as part of School Y's annual report to the school board.

Team Attitude

- Team members cooperated.
- Team members shared information.

- Team members were committed to the team goals.
- Team members showed respect for one another.

Now, the A-Team needs to determine an appropriate rating scale, the number of levels, and the anchor points for each level. The team opts for a 5-point scale: 1 = completely disagree, 2 = disagree somewhat, 3 = neither agree nor disagree, 4 = agree somewhat, 5 = completely agree.

The next issue to resolve is who will be rating the team's performance on each dimension. After examining each of the components, it becomes clear that the A-Team members and the A-Team coach are best able to rate the team on its performance.

The final concern to be discussed is the purpose or purposes for which the evaluation is to be used. In this case, the evaluation arouses little apprehension. The members all volunteered for the task, and they are not being paid for their time. However, the A-Team does view the evaluation as useful because the task is only partially completed. The team will use the information to make some decisions about whether it should continue as it has been working or if it should make some changes. In addition, the A-Team evaluation will be fed back to the school board at the conclusion of the entire process as part of the board's overall evaluation of the accountability initiative.

Thus, a meeting is called just to go through the A-Team's evaluation. The principal and president of the parent association are invited to observe this meeting. They agree, and their attendance reinforces the A-Team members' perception that an evaluation of their performance is important.

Before the meeting, the coach writes down all of the components on a flip chart. At the start of the meeting, he distributes the rating forms. All members complete the forms, as does the coach. After the forms are filled out, the coach collects them and puts up all the members' ratings alongside each component. Subsequent discussion by all individuals present goes into discrepancies in ratings and possible explanations for them, ratings of 3 or lower and how to improve them, and ratings of 4 or 5 in celebration of a job well done. In addition, similarities and discrepancies between coach and member ratings are discussed.

This case is an example of how to carry out a team performance evaluation. Following are a few highlights:

First, note that the five standard dimensions for the team's performance were all relevant; what changed was the wording and composition of the components. This is typical. The dimensions of performance tend to generalize across organizations although the components within each dimension are likely to be highly variable from team to team. For example, it is unlikely that the components of being an effective team teacher are the same as being an effective team computer programmer or team garbage collector. Thus, when the team has input in determining the components on which it will be evaluated, members have a much higher level of commitment to the evaluation process and are less likely to circumvent or sabotage it.

Second, the assignment of a coach was a wise move by the school board. Because the teams for the various schools were likely to be made up of individuals unfamiliar with teamwork, a coach would facilitate it. In addition, the coach would likely know how to get the team working on task.

Third, the raters for the components were the coach and the team members, not the principal or others. This arrangement, though appropriate for the A-Team, is not typical. For most teams, supervisors, external customers, and internal customers may be in a position to evaluate the team's performance.

Fourth, the task force was given the time frame but little other direction in conducting the work. Thus, the task was a very difficult one. Interim feedback on its own performance is an excellent way to ensure that a team stays on track.

This case demonstrates that it is possible, and useful, to set up an evaluation system for almost any type of team. Although the process takes time to think and work through, providing performance feedback to teams will result in high-performing and more effective teams.

Importance of Performance Feedback

A system to evaluate the observable aspects of team performance is essential. Teams want and need performance evaluation feedback if they are to function effectively. Although it takes some time to set up a system that teams can live with, it is worth the effort.

CHAPTER TEN

EVALUATING TEAM AND MEMBER SATISFACTION

Much attention has always focused on the observable outcomes of performance, whether that performance is at the individual or the team level. This focus makes intuitive sense, in that productivity and the bottom line are usually highly relevant aspects of overall organizational performance. For teams, however, other important aspects of performance should be evaluated as well. These aspects of performance touch on the human side of teams.

Differentiating Team and Member Satisfaction

How often have you worked on a team where the outcome was highly successful (or even moderately successful), but you could hardly wait for the task to end because you never wanted to see the other members of the team again, or because the task was so unrewarding personally that you never wanted to be associated with it again? If you are like most of us who work in organizations in which teams or committees are a way of life, the answer, unfortunately, is, "All too often."

Researchers have recognized that it is important to evaluate not only the outputs of the team but also the team as a team. That is, the team that manages to produce successful work might be rotting from the inside out. If it is important for organizations to have team members who feel successful and enjoy working in teams, then it is certainly worthwhile to evaluate these aspects of teamwork so that interventions can occur before the team self-destructs.

One might argue that the satisfaction of the team and its members is irrelevant, but that approach is shortsighted. For example, if a task force is only together for a defined period of time and the members don't get along, it is easy to conclude that it really doesn't matter if the team members hate one another by the time the project ends. But what if another task force is created, and two people from the previous one are elected to serve on the new task force? Clearly, there will be a problem with the new task force. Another potential problem may arise if the members of a standing team are highly dissatisfied with the work they do. Although the team may be able to produce high-quality work for a period of time, over the long term the members may not only quit the team but quit the organization altogether!

Two aspects of the team's satisfaction, then, are worth monitoring from an organizational health perspective: the satisfaction of individual members working as part of a particular team, and the extent to which the team members want to work together as a unit in the future. The notion that there are two aspects of satisfaction is supported by Sundstrom, DeMeuse, and Futrell (1990) when they describe team viability as encompassing both the team members' satisfaction and their willingness to continue working together. For Sundstrom, DeMeuse, and Futrell, overall viability combines the two. Hackman (1987) preferred to keep these constructs distinct in his model, so that the satisfaction of team members as individuals and the willingness of the members to work together in the future were separate aspects of overall team effectiveness. I agree with Hackman's approach. Although the two are probably related, from a diagnostic and interventionist perspective it is better to keep the two distinct. Thus, in this chapter, member satisfaction and team satisfaction are treated as two different factors.

Member Satisfaction

Member satisfaction refers to an individual team member's degree of satisfaction at being part of a specific team. Each team member may feel different levels of satisfaction with how well the team facilitates his or her personal goals, how the team is led, how the team makes decisions, and so on.

Member satisfaction is different from job satisfaction and is a relatively new construct. However, it seems reasonable to postulate that a pattern of relationships, similar to those with job satisfaction, will emerge from member satisfaction. So what are the relationships that we know about from the job satisfaction literature that we might be able to generalize to the member satisfaction construct?

First, there is no established link between job satisfaction and worker productivity. In other words, happy workers are not necessarily more productive workers; productivity depends on much more than just a happy workforce. Second, job satisfaction *is* related to other important variables, such as commitment to the organization and going above and beyond the call of duty in everyday tasks.

It is important to distinguish between job satisfaction and member satisfaction. Job satisfaction is more concerned with the individually determined aspects of a job or position. Feelings of job satisfaction frequently relate to such factors as task variety, skill use, and pay, which are associated within a specified role or job description. Job satisfaction is a construct that has been described and measured for years. In contrast, member satisfaction has to do with the aspects of being part of a team. Because it is a very new concept, there are few tools available to evaluate it.

A few examples of the evaluation of member satisfaction are emerging from the research literature. For example, Watson, Michaelson, and Sharp (1991) found that, over time, one of the important aspects of satisfaction for individual team members is the extent to which working with a particular team helps the member to achieve personal goals. Witteman (1991) proposed that group member satisfaction is important along three dimensions: satisfaction with how decisions are made within the group, communication between group members, and group leadership. Yeatts and Hyten (1998) have suggested that a useful question to ask of team members is, "Do you like working on a team, or would you prefer going back to having a supervisor?" (p. 318). Finally, Hallam and Campbell (1997) have created the Team Development Survey, which includes items that measure individual goals and satisfaction. In all this literature, some common themes may be useful in evaluating member satisfaction (see Exhibit 10.1).

Notice that the items pertain to the specific team on which the members are currently working. Thus, the member satisfaction instrument differs substantially from the ten-item Team Player Inventory (Kline, 1999b) discussed in Chapter Six. Recall that the TPI measures a general positive or negative predisposition toward teamwork *in general*, whereas the set of six items in Exhibit 10.1 relate to member satisfaction with working on *a particular team*.

Team Satisfaction

The construct of team satisfaction is also relatively recent. Its relationship to other variables of interest, such as team performance or organizational commitment, has yet to be demonstrated. Still, evaluating the extent to which team members are willing to work together in the future does seem to be important. A low degree of

EXHIBIT 10.1. MEASURING MEMBER SATISFACTION.

These items are completed by team members individually. Read each item and determine the extent to which you agree with it. Interpretation of the scores is provided after the items.

	Completely disagree	Disagree somewhat	Neither agree nor disagree	Agree somewhat	Completely agree
1. I am satisfied with the way this team enhances my personal career goals.	1	2	3	4	5
2. I am satisfied with the way this team enhances my personal job satisfaction.	1	2	3	4	5
3. I am satisfied with the way this team makes decisions.	1	2	3	4	5
4. I am satisfied with how my skills are used in this team's work.	1	2	3	4	5
5. I am satisfied with how this team is led.	1	2	3	4	5
6. I am satisfied with my input into the team's work.	1	2	3	4	5

Note: When interpreting scores for the member satisfaction scale, average the responses for each individual over the number of items to which the person responded. The reason for doing this is that an individual may not answer all the questions, as all of them may not be relevant. For example, item 5 on team leadership may be irrelevant to self-managed work teams with no identifiable leader. In this case the responses to items 1 to 4 are added together and then divided by five to come up with an average value.

The scores range from a low of 1 to a high of 5. Member satisfaction scores in the 1 to 2 range would be considered low, member satisfaction around 3 would be considered average, and member satisfaction scores in the 4 to 5 range would be considered high.

willingness means the organization is going to have a lot of trouble with its teams, and the effects are likely to be felt in the short term. Conversely, when there is a high degree of willingness the outlook for creating new teams and continuing with team initiatives in the organization is much more positive.

Few attempts have been made actually to measure this construct. Yeatts and Hyten (1998) suggest that team members should be asked a rather lengthy question about the conditions that might cause the team to perform poorly or break down. Using a different approach, Watson, Michaelson, and Sharp (1991) devised a set of questions, called the Group-Interaction Measure, which they adapted from other sources.

The Group-Interaction items seem to tap into the construct of team satisfaction and have the virtue of being much briefer than the question posed by Yeatts and Hyten. Unfortunately, Watson, Michaelson, and Sharp used them in a classroom context, which means they need to be adapted further in order to be useful in an organizational context. In addition, these researchers' interest in the measurement of group interaction was its effects over the long term with scores on a standardized test, not in the measurement of team satisfaction as defined in this chapter. Thus, I have modified the items to measure team satisfaction better and more directly (see Exhibit 10.2).

Team members' responses to these questions will provide the organization with an idea of how likely its teams are to remain intact and also to be successful in the future.

The following case study demonstrates how to use the information collected from the member and team satisfaction scales.

Case Study: Using the Member and Team Satisfaction Measures

Firm X is a medium-size accounting firm with a traditional bureaucracy governing its structure and function. More than five hundred employees work for Firm X, and they are divided into several different departments. Each department has multiple units, and there are several teams within units. Firm X has recently downsized its staff through attrition; that is, it will not replace those workers who retire in an effort to hold costs in check without having to resort to layoffs.

The team approach has been in effect for about nine months. Firm X's CEO believes strongly that a team-based approach to the traditional hierarchy is a good way to deal with the decrease in the number of employees.

Some of the teams seem to be doing fine, but others are obviously floundering. There is a considerable amount of unrest at the senior executive meetings, with some department heads calling for an end to the team approach and others embracing it.

EXHIBIT 10.2. MEASURING TEAM SATISFACTION.

These items are completed by team members individually. Read each item and determine the extent to which you agree with it. Interpretation of the scores is provided after the items.

	Completely disagree	Disagree somewhat	Neither agree nor disagree	Agree somewhat	Completely agree
1. I like working with the individuals who are on my present team.	1	2	3	4	5
2. Compared with other teams I have worked on, this team works well together.	1	2	3	4	5
3. I prefer working with this team rather than by myself.	1	2	3	4	5
4. I would not pursue an opportunity to leave this team and work on another.	1	2	3	4	5
5. I look forward to working with my present team members in the future.	1	2	3	4	5
6. My team emphasizes the team's goals.	1	2	3	4	5

Note: When interpreting scores for the team satisfaction scale, average the responses for each individual over the number of items to which the person responded. The reason for doing this is that an individual may not answer all the questions, as all of them may not be relevant. For example, item 5 on looking forward to working with present team members in the future may be irrelevant for student project teams where members will graduate and never see each other again. In this case the responses to items 1 to 4 and 6 are added together and then divided by five to come up with an average value.

The scores range from a low of 1 to a high of 5. Team satisfaction scores in the 1 to 2 range would be considered low, team satisfaction around 3 would be considered average, and team satisfaction scores in the 4 to 5 range would be considered high.

The CEO goes to the director of the human resources department with a query about what to do. The director suggests evaluating all teams in terms of both member and team satisfaction to provide some baseline information about which teams are likely to have problems and which ones are not. The CEO agrees, and the survey is conducted.

Specifically, the HR director asks each team member to complete the six-item member satisfaction and the six-item team satisfaction scales. Members are to identify the team to which they belong but give no other individual identifying information; the hope is that anonymity will encourage them to be honest in their assessments.

The average scores of the teams are computed across all team members, yielding a single team value for the satisfaction scales. A partial set of the responses is shown in Exhibit 10.3.

Several noteworthy observations can be gleaned from this information. First, note that the clerical unit teams (A, D, G, and J) are all fairly low on member satisfaction. The team concept apparently is not working for clerical staff as far as furthering their own personal goals, and they don't particularly like the way their teams operate. This group of employees is also low on team satisfaction. Clearly, from these two pieces of data one can make a strong case that some sort of team intervention is needed for the clerical staff. It might be that the clerical tasks of Firm X simply do not lend themselves to a team approach. Perhaps certain individuals within the clerical staff will just not cooperate. There could be any of a variety of reasons for the low scores. However, Firm X would be wise to initiate some sort of intervention, because clerical staff are deemed to be an integral part of the organization and they clearly need some help. The first step would be to ask these team members why their satisfaction is so low.

The next issue of note is that two finance teams have a fairly high level of team satisfaction coupled with a moderate level of member satisfaction. This high level of team

EXHIBIT 10.3. RESULTS OF THE TEAM AND MEMBER SATISFACTION ASSESSMENTS.

Department	Unit	Team	Member Satisfaction	Team Satisfaction
Finance	Clerical	A	1.7	2.0
Finance	Law	B	3.5	4.6
Finance	Banking	C	3.8	4.5
Marketing	Clerical	D	2.0	2.4
Marketing	Research	E	4.9	4.7
Marketing	Promotion	F	4.7	4.8
Client Service	Clerical	G	1.5	2.1
Client Service	Business	H	3.0	3.1
Client Service	Personal Tax	I	2.8	2.9
Human Resources	Clerical	J	1.8	2.2
Human Resources	Staffing	K	4.2	2.1
Human Resources	Employee Assistance	L	4.5	1.8

satisfaction should be celebrated and recognized by Firm X. In addition, asking team members why their team satisfaction is so high will provide some clues about how to help other, less satisfied teams become more satisfied. Perhaps lower member satisfaction is because the finance department is set up in such a way that personal goals cannot be readily achieved.

For the client services teams, both member and team satisfaction are at moderate levels. Perhaps those in client services don't see much change in their working lives as a result of the team initiative—they can take it or leave it. A couple of interventions—to make the individual worker input seen to be valuable both by the individual and by other team members—might be worth a try. Making the teams more cohesive would be helpful as well; one way to do this would be for senior management to recognize the teams as teams.

Another interesting set of data relates to the teams in human resources. Although two have high levels of member satisfaction, their team satisfaction is comparatively low. These groups are worth examining more closely. In this department, there seems to be the general feeling that the work each individual puts into the team is worthwhile, but the members would prefer to have different coworkers. A potentially helpful intervention might either shift these teams' members around or work to make the teams more cohesive.

The final teams to note are two marketing teams, which have high levels of both member and team satisfaction. From a developmental standpoint, it would be worth asking these teams why they seem to have been so successful in embracing the team initiative. Assistance for other teams could be generated from the information they provide.

This case study demonstrates how team and member satisfaction can be assessed. It also shows why a firm would be interested in carrying out the work. Team initiatives are not welcomed by employees these days. Evaluations of team and member satisfaction might shed some light on why this is so in a particular organization and how the organization might make team initiatives into a more positive experience for all employees.

Importance of Team and Member Satisfaction

The importance of evaluating teams cannot be overstated. It is an integral part of the team-building process. Without evaluation, teams do not know how they are performing, key issues such as whether the team will work together in the future cannot be assessed, and there is no way to tie the team's performance to any valued outcomes, such as bonuses or promotions.

It is easy to understand why, as a general rule, organizations have not engaged in team evaluation. First, thinking about and using the team rather than the individual as the work unit is still a relatively recent phenomenon. There is a high degree of uncertainty about the best way to evaluate teams. Few validated measures of team performance have been generated by the academic community; furthermore, there is virtually no experience with team evaluation in the work world—let alone any approaches that might be called best practices. Second, individual evaluations are often resented or avoided because of the hard feelings they can engender. There is an expectation that evaluating teams will only compound these negative aspects of performance evaluation.

All too often, therefore, teams are left to fend for themselves to determine how well they are performing. This is not enough. Although informal self-feedback is a start, all of us need performance feedback that comes from external sources.

Teams need a way to evaluate aspects of performance outcomes that includes both self and external feedback (see Chapter Nine). In addition, teams need a way to evaluate team satisfaction and individual member satisfaction. By using the provided assessment tools, an organization can begin a systematic evaluation program for its own teams.

CHAPTER ELEVEN

TECHNOLOGY AND VIRTUAL TEAMS

Up to this point, the ideas and cases put forward have treated teams as if they all operated traditionally. The teams are located together geographically and the members interact face-to-face. In fact, however, many organizations have teams whose members are dispersed. They may be located across the country or across the ocean and so be geographically dispersed. They may work different shifts and so be temporally dispersed. No book on team performance can ignore the technological advancements made over the past several years that deal with dispersed teams—or, as they are often called, *virtual teams*. The effectiveness of these advancements, however, is still open to question.

Technology and Teams

Early work that systematically examined the effects of technology on organizations shows that it was treated primarily as a way to restructure the organization's work. That is, technological effects on the organization's structure were the primary focus, and its effects on productivity were largely ignored (Goodman, 1986). This trend continues today. The uses to which the newest technology is put, and the resultant effects on how it will change the organization's structure, are described in great detail. What is lacking is a clear message about how the technology is actually used and how it helps (or hinders) both individual and team effectiveness.

This kind of omission is unusual when we remember that technology is often introduced ostensibly to improve productivity, quality, or both. Methot and Phillips-Grant (1998) point out that these hoped-for effects are only sometimes realized. They note that organizations benefit most from technological innovations when they are part of an overall, larger scheme that introduces changes in human resources and work processes as well as the tools to carry out the work.

Groupware: The Technology That Assists Virtual Teams

The term used to describe the computer technology that has been created to facilitate collaborating users, including virtual teams, is *groupware* (Krasner, McInroy, & Walz, 1991). Groupware consists not just of the newest technology—such as screen-sharing software, group decision support systems, and collaborative authoring tools—but also e-mail, electronic bulletin boards, teleconferencing systems, and videoconferencing systems (Greenburg, 1991). When these new tools originally hit the market, they were greeted with great enthusiasm. Claims of improvement in areas such as team communication, planning, idea generating, problem solving, negotiation, collaborative document preparation, and decision quality were rampant (for example, Valacich, Dennis, & Nunamaker, 1991; Thornton & Lockhart, 1994). Even more recently, Townsend, DeMarie, and Hendrickson (1998) posit that virtual teams will assist organizations in becoming strategically flexible in an increasingly competitive marketplace.

To balance these optimistic projections, several writers who have actually taken a look at groupware systems in organizations have found that these gains are not likely to accrue (Grudin, 1994; Hildebrand, 1996; King, 1996). The collection of case studies by Ciborra (1996) highlights the fact that groupware can have unexpected consequences for teamwork, many of them negative. These less-than-flattering findings are not surprising; early on, Goodman (1986) noted that technology places *constraints* on teams and their work; it does not free them. In fact, in his definition of technology, Goodman explicitly states that there are constraining components within any technological system: "Technology is a system of components directly involved in acting on and/or changing an object from one state to another" (p. 139). These constraining components are revisited later in this chapter, after what is known about groupware is discussed.

Groupware: The Evidence

There have been a couple of recent reviews of the literature on groupware systems (Hollingshead & McGrath, 1995; Kline & McGrath, forthcoming). Both indicate that the effects of groupware on teamwork are highly speculative. The Kline and McGrath review encompassed a variety of groupware technologies. We concluded that most of the studies on group effectiveness shared four weaknesses: they were based on laboratory studies, they used group decision support systems almost exclusively, they did not include reference to the contextual variables that have been so important in traditional teamwork, and they failed to define effectiveness in a manner that would make the findings generalize to other samples.

Hollingshead and McGrath focused only on fifty studies that have used group decision support systems. Despite restricting their review to these studies alone, Hollingshead and McGrath came to conclusions similar to ours. First, because the studies were based on ad hoc groups brought together for one session, any findings are not likely to hold up in the real world. Second, these studies virtually ignored contextual, group, and member characteristics; the attention of the researchers focused only on the decision technology; and other variables were lumped together as leftover error variance. Third, there was a confounding of communication system type, task type, and research strategy across studies.

Certainly there is a need for a more systematic program of research on groupware. This research needs to be driven by some theoretical framework, be carried out longitudinally, and collect data with actual teams that function in actual contexts.

But are there things that are known about virtual teams and groupware that will facilitate teams right now? Can some light be shed on how to make better use of groupware systems? The answer to both questions is, tentatively, yes.

Principles to Make Groupware Effective

This section presents a synthesis of information retrieved from a number of sources: reading the accumulated wisdom based on existing research (for example, Goodman, 1986; Hollingshead & McGrath, 1995; Kline & Gardiner, 1997; Methot & Phillips-Grant, 1998; Townsend, DeMarie, & Hendrickson, 1998), watching users of groupware systems, and holding discussions with groupware researchers who are at the cutting edge of their research fields. Clearly, there are some principles to adhere to when implementing any groupware system.

The question of how best to present these principles in some organized manner recalls Goodman's (1986) listing of four constraints within any technological system, all of which can either contribute to or detract from a team's effectiveness. These were *equipment* (both hardware and software); *materials* (objects being worked on, such as a collaborative document or ideas generated to solve problems); *physical environment* (where the action takes place—in groupware, it is somewhere in cyberspace); and *programs* (rules and procedures invoked to get the work accomplished). The degree to which each of these groupware components is compatible with the team and its tasks will determine its impact on the team's effectiveness. Each will be discussed in turn.

Equipment

Teams report that the primary reason why software is used is that it is user-friendly. The less intuitive the procedures are, the less likely any system is to be adopted. This phenomenon is highlighted in the example of videoconferencing systems. In many organizations, people report that prime office space has been allocated for a room that is hardly used. The reason is that the technology is complex to learn and cumbersome to operate. Even executives, who have the resources at their disposal to get someone else to set up and run the technological aspects of a videoconference, rarely use the system.

The same holds true of other groupware software systems—even simple e-mail systems, for example, which many professionals now depend on. It took a period of time before anyone used them with any degree of comfort. With the newer e-mail interfaces, which tend to be more user-friendly, more and more people are likely to use and indeed do use the programs.

Principle One: Before purchasing a groupware system, ask to try it out. Make sure that the end users can readily use it. Go to the extreme of taking them along on the purchasing expedition.

The other equipment issue is the hardware. This issue is frequently brought forward as a complaint by system users. The problems of system unreliability (it breaks down) as well as insufficient power (bandwidth, RAM speed, and so on) are obvious constraints to any system's effective use. This issue is exacerbated in groupware systems because by definition there must be at least two (and usually more) stations running simultaneously. If any one of them breaks down, the communication is severed.

Track records of different groupware systems are available for the asking—you just have to remember to ask the vendor to see them! The other, more fruitful method of ferreting out this information comes from personnel who *actually use* the system, not just those who purchase it. They can provide a wealth of information about how their organization ended up using (or not using) the system.

Principle Two: Find out the reliability and capacity of the groupware system you are interested in to determine if it meets your needs.

Materials

In groupware systems the objects may be collaborative documents, such as reports or proposals. They may be graphic displays, such as building diagrams or newspaper layouts. They may even be the records containing all of the ideas generated in a brainstorming exercise. They are analogous to the outputs that would result from any traditional face-to-face team meeting.

There is a high degree of constraint when working on objects across space, time, or both with a team of people. An elaborate protocol system needs to be understood and used. A primary issue is that of ensuring that appropriate "turn-taking" protocol has been established.

For example, let's say a research and development (R&D) team working on developing a new antipsychotic drug is charged with writing an interim report on its work to date. This report will be read by the firm's executives, so it must be compelling and concise. The team works in different offices around the company's property, so members use a document-sharing groupware system. This system allows all members of the team to see the same document at the same time and have input into it simultaneously, so members need not plan face-to-face meetings.

Team Member 1 is designated to provide a draft of an outline as a starting point to the groupware session where the purpose is to complete the outline of the report. Team Member 2 (previously designated) makes an edit to the outline. Then Team Member 3 (again, already designated) makes another edit. Team Member 4 takes a turn, and so it continues until all edits to the outline have been completed. The team is now ready to move on to the next part of the report writing. At this juncture, assignments for completing certain sections of the report are given to the various team members, and another series of groupware meetings is set up to edit each of the sections. Obviously, even from this relatively simple example, it becomes clear that the groupware approach is more constraining than working in a face-to-face setting. Although the task of editing the outline is possible, it takes more time than the R&D team anticipated.

From this illustration, it can be seen that not all tasks will lend themselves well to a groupware situation. The materials associated with tasks that require a free-flowing, ad hoc, interactive approach from all team members at the same time will not work well. For example, imagine the task of a team charged with developing an advertising campaign for a politician. The team members work in different offices across the country, so they have to arrange meetings that take into account the various time zones in which people work. They set up a groupware meeting to brainstorm about how to get the politician elected. This team happens to have some of the latest technology, allowing the members to log onto their personal computers and see video images of the other team members, hear voices of the other team members, and input information into their computer via their keyboard. A log is kept of the written computer transactions.

Members of the advertising team may feel that they want to speak quickly and use gestures to make a point, but they are slowed down so that the instrument that records the team's work can keep up. They may need to read the body language of the other team members as they try out ideas, but the video images that come across on their computer display are too grainy to do it easily. The team members may be in the habit of jumping in to build on an idea just generated, but they may be out of turn in the groupware system. As a result, the team decides that everyone needs to get on planes and meet one another in one location one day next week.

This example illustrates something that we (Kline & Gardiner, 1997) came across in our interviews with groupware users. The participants reported that although travel costs to the organization were supposed to be cut by using the groupware, often they were not. Some materials and tasks are simply not amenable to anything except face-to-face teamwork.

Principle Three: The task and the materials to be used for the task or resulting from the task must be amenable to being performed effectively in a groupware system.

Researchers have known for decades that the technology used must be compatible with the work to be accomplished by the team (for example, Hickson, Pugh, & Pheysey, 1969; Perrow, 1967; Thompson, 1967; Woodward, 1965). The advertising campaign example was not amenable to groupware mediation. However, a different task with different materials—such as editing a final version of a report—may very well lend itself to groupware-mediated work, and save the dispersed team some time as well!

Physical Environment

The issue of physical space may seem to be largely irrelevant for teams using groupware technology, but it is not. By way of example, let's return to the R&D team working on the outline of its report. Some of the limitations associated with the task include not being able to hear or see the other team members. Although some advancements in the field have allowed for voice and even video images to accompany the voices in a groupware meeting, problems arise as a result. Specifically, the concern about screen space becomes paramount. If an image of a person is in the corner of your screen, the document or display layout in that section is no longer visible. For the R&D team, the size of the outline is a problem because of its length. It is impossible to see the whole outline at the same time. Because of this restriction, it is difficult to move one section spontaneously to another to reorganize the outline. All team members are limited to looking at the same part of the outline as the member who is working on the document. Other members have to wait until it is their turn to move the cursor.

Principle Four: The physical environment that will display the interactions between team members must be sufficiently large to allow the task to be completed.

So the physical environment *is* a concern even for the most simple groupware systems. As the systems become more complex, the ways in which the physical environment can be constraining increase as well. For example, in a videoconferencing system, two office locations must be permanently available to house the equipment. Space designated just for this purpose takes up a lot of office real estate that could be more efficiently used. Videoconference rooms can be shared with other workers, but that means that videoconferencing will be further restricted to the times when no one else is using the rooms.

Another example of this occurs with the use of electronic whiteboards. These devices record the documented interactions of face-to-face meetings. They are essentially flip charts that allow the contents of a meeting to be printed off and thus become part of the documented work of the team. Often the conference rooms that house these boards are coveted by many teams, and booking them becomes a problem. These physical space issues gives rise to Principle Five.

Principle Five: For teams interacting in physical locations, the rooms must be available for use on a regular basis.

Programs

The rules and procedures to be followed when using many groupware systems are very elaborate. They are elaborate because team members' time (particularly if they are in different time zones), computing time, and office space are all at a premium. As a result, those who use groupware find that it is best to structure groupware-mediated meetings as much as possible.

Setting up the meeting well in advance, sending around the meeting agenda and then sticking to it, ensuring that all members know the turn-taking protocol that will be used (whether it be vocal or via keyboard stroking) are all things that facilitate the effectiveness of these types of meetings. Notice what is absent from these structured meetings: spontaneous interaction between team members. There is an inverse relationship between the number of rules and procedures to be followed and the amount of room left over for flexibility and creativity.

Therefore, determine the extent to which the task will call for a creative and flexible work environment. If it is necessary, then the team will probably benefit from meeting face-to-face. If the meeting is well suited to working in a highly structured environment, then groupware-mediated meetings are much more likely to be received positively by the users.

Principle Six: The inverse relationship between the number of rules and procedures and the ability of the team to be flexible and creative should assist in determining if a groupware-mediated meeting is appropriate.

Further Guidelines

The constraints suggested by Goodman (1986) provide a useful way to conceptualize some of the concerns around using groupware technology. Kline and Gardiner (1997) have identified other issues that organizations often fail to take into account when launching into any new technology, not just groupware technology. The following guidelines reflect what we found.

Guideline One: Assume that the up-front costs associated with purchasing any technological system will be higher than expected.

Usually the technology deliverer also is contracted to help set up the system in the organization and to train at least some key personnel in its use. This cost is often not part of the price of the software and hardware needed.

Guideline Two: Assume that the secondary costs associated with purchasing any technological system will be higher than expected.

Often organizations find out after they have purchased the new technology that the present electrical wiring in the building is not sufficient. They also may find out that new space is needed, so they have to lease more or renovate what they have to accommodate the technology.

Guideline Three: Remember that there is a learning curve when any new technology is introduced.

In other words, there will be some downtime for employees as they learn the new system and make mistakes. Accounting for downtime is an absolute must. The most consistent theme we heard from users was that they never had the chance to learn the new system appropriately. They went through a lot of trial and error to learn to do it right. They used other employees' experiences to help them along. There was no systematic training effort on the part of the organization. Somehow, the employees were supposed to be up and running with the new technology overnight, but it didn't happen.

Guideline Four: Provide sufficient start-up training on the new technology.

This guideline builds directly on the previous one. The more formal training provided, the less downtime for the organization in the longer run.

Guideline Five: Provide sufficient and ongoing user help.

There is getting to be more and more of a market for technophiles who know how to use technological systems. Most organizations find that they need to hire new personnel just to handle the incoming calls associated with problems experienced by users. Assistance needs are especially acute if employees can work at home and need to get help in the evenings or on weekends.

Guideline Six: Remember that the new groupware technology is not an answer to a strategic problem.

The new technology is a set of tools that enable teams to work more effectively in some situations. It seems most fruitful, then, to talk about any technology, including groupware, as a tool. Groupware is a means to an end, not an end in itself. Thus, the task to be accomplished by the team can never be uncoupled from the groupware technology that is supposed to make the team more effective. In some situations, as we have seen, groupware may help. In some instances, groupware is so limiting that it hinders the team.

Conclusions on Groupware and Team Effectiveness

This discussion of groupware could have been introduced at the points where the Team Performance Model refers to task issues. Those issues include the determination of the type of team, the match between the way the team is structured and the tasks it is expected to perform, and the articulation and sharing of the team's goals by all members. Each team needs to come to a consensus on how and when to use groupware technology to facilitate its work. If the decision is based on the team's purpose and tasks, then the decision will be a good one. If it is forced on the team, or if the team decides to use a technology simply because it looks interesting, then the decision will likely prove to be regrettable.

Groupware systems should be purchased with the idea that they are to solve a specific team problem or because the team's tasks can obviously benefit from the technology. The systems should not be introduced simply because the firm next door did so; they are just too costly to justify such an approach.

Finally, organizations that have offices in other countries or perhaps want to become partners with firms in other countries need to be especially cautious about the extent to which groupware is used. This caution is necessary because many cultures assume that a bond of personal trust must be developed between the high-ranking officers of companies before any business will be conducted. That is, the person with whom you do business needs to have a name, a face, and a personality; you need to feel you can trust him. This trust can be gained only through face-to-face meetings. These meetings have a tendency to be quite lengthy, and there are frequently many of them. This approach is quite different from the more impersonal interactions that characterize North American business. In these situations, groupware cannot be a substitute.

In closing, there are still many issues to be resolved—both generally and specifically with each team—before any implementation of groupware systems for virtual teams will be predictably successful.

CHAPTER TWELVE

WRAPPING UP

It would be futile and unproductive to reiterate all of the various lessons I have learned about teams and teamwork and have tried to include in the previous eleven chapters. Instead, in this chapter my purpose is to do three things: present the best take-home messages that can be derived from this book as a whole, describe what I believe to be the most pressing issues facing teams in organizational contexts, and highlight what I believe to be the critical theoretical and empirical issues that team researchers face.

The prescriptions and thoughts presented in this chapter are not based only on my own work and observation. Instead, they draw on the wisdom and writings of many authors over the past two decades, including Baker and Salas (1997), Guzzo (1995b), McGrath (1986), Mohrman, Cohen, and Mohrman (1995), Nurick (1982), Tjosvold (1986), Varney (1989), and Wellins, Byham, and Wilson (1991).

Take-Home Messages

Successful teams are not built overnight. They are not achieved in a weekend retreat. They are achieved when the context is one that supports them, when the tasks are ones that team members can and do accomplish, when success is clearly articulated and celebrated, and when success is felt by the team members. These processes take a lot of work on the part of the organization as well as on the part of the team members. Teams that are put together with little planning, few resources, and little support are not going to result in an organizational advantage. Thus, team building is a destination that, for many organizations, is not worth the trip. For those organizations that do plan to embark on the journey and for those that have begun it, this book should provide some help in making teams successful.

By way of providing a coherent whole, recall the Team Performance Model from Chapter One around which this book was organized. Using this model as a template, if I were going to create a team-based organization, I would deal with the eighteen issues outlined in the following paragraphs, which I believe are the most pressing ones facing teams in organizational contexts.

This list is not comprehensive; nor would any of its points likely be discounted as irrelevant by most team researchers or practitioners. The list highlights the complexities of having successful teams in organizational contexts. It forces organizations to think through the team notion systematically, with an eye to what kind of changes this approach may actually mean for the organization.

This list of eighteen pressing issues is based on my Team Performance Model. Despite the complex nature of the model, teams and team performance are actually even more complex. For example, the team's level of performance feeds right back into resources teams need, team characteristics, and work process effectiveness. These feedback loops are not shown in the model for two reasons. The first is that the model is complex enough as it is. The second is that we are just beginning to understand how the feedback loops work (for example, West, 1998). It is important to note, though, that these feedback loops do exist; teams that perform well are likely to begin a cycle of success, and those that perform poorly are likely to begin a cycle of failure. (See again Figure 1.1.)

Practical Team Issues

Organizations did not increase their use of teams by chance, nor are teams an initiative spurred on by management's wanting to meet the social needs of employees. Teams have been formed in reaction to the practical reality that organizations have become flatter and smaller. The result is that personnel are required to take on new responsibilities and a broader range of them. Jobs have become more complex and managers have to deal with new types of communication issues (Berwald, 1998). Out of this reality come six issues that organizations are dealing with right now as they move into team-based work environments.

EXHIBIT 12.1. A TEMPLATE FOR MAKING TEAMS EFFECTIVE.

1. Determine the purpose of the organization. Without a clear overarching purpose, no human resource initiative, team-based or otherwise, is going to work. Making the vision clear, so that all organizational members can understand it, is critical. This purpose will become even more critical at a later stage, when the team members must adopt the organizational goals as their own.

2. Determine whether teams are necessary to accomplish the organization's work. Any team initiative should be part of the organization's overall business strategy. The time and effort needed to build effective teams may not be necessary and may even be counterproductive. For some organizations where members work almost on their own, forcing a team approach onto the structure is inappropriate.

3. If teams are the way to go, determine if they are going to act like crews, task forces, standing teams, or some combination. Each type of team requires some unique team-building work. For example, training a standing team to deal with the kinds of issues that task forces cope with (for example, how to make sure that a project ends on time) is not a good use of time.

4. Ensure that the teams know the criteria on which their performance will be evaluated. These criteria will likely vary from organization to organization and even from team to team within the same organization. Members who know what they are expected to do are much more likely to do it. Although ensuring that teams know what is expected of them may seem an obvious technique, the unfortunate reality is that most teams do not have explicit performance criteria.

5. Ensure that all team members know and understand the team's goals. This suggestion is a corollary to the preceding one, in that the goals may easily tie into the performance expectations. However, the goal-setting process ensures that the team is very familiar with all of the subgoals and time lines of the team. Explicit goals also help to ensure that the team's goals are in alignment with the organization's goals.

6. Ensure that each team member knows his or her role in accomplishing the team's goals.

7. Require teams to write a resource plan for physical, financial, human, and time needs over a specified period of time (one year, for example). In writing the plan, the teams are forced to document what they are going to do, who is going to do it, how it will be accomplished; the plan therefore provides a rationale for determining resource allocation decisions by the organization.

8. Provide the necessary training to team leaders so that they can play a supportive role for the teams. This often proves to be difficult because part of the training needs to be assisting leaders to shed the traditional leader functions of controlling and planning. These functions have been shifted to the team. Instead, team leaders need to perform functions they have never been trained to handle—such as liaison, resource procurement, and conflict resolution, to name a few.

9. Provide a supportive context for the teams. Conduct team evaluations rather than just individual evaluations, ensure that the organization recognizes the teams, locate teams together geographically, acknowledge team outputs publicly, and ensure that teams know how their work fits into the organization's overall plan.

10. Provide the opportunity for team efficacy to flourish. In order for this to happen, the team will need to work on challenging tasks and execute them well. Team members will need to see themselves as the ones responsible for their success. Teams will need to be recognized by the organization as a success.

11. Play down the role of personality conflicts or personality differences in any team-building exercises. Instead, get members to focus on the tasks at hand. When an individual

EXHIBIT 12.1. (*continued*)

is disruptive to the team, that person needs to be dealt with immediately by a supervisor who has position power over him or her.

12. Take careful account of the skills that each member brings to the team; each member's skills should be used in team tasks. Skills of each member should be increased systematically so that redundancy is built into the team. This is not just good practice for teams; it is also good management practice in general to have employees capable of taking on diverse roles.

13. Train the teams to hold effective meetings.

14. Ensure that teams have a mechanism to make decisions in a way that makes them acceptable to all team members, and also defensible to people external to the team.

15. Train teams to manage conflict before they begin to work. If conflict is a problem for the team, be prepared to provide assistance.

16. Evaluate teams regularly (and new teams, frequently). Provide developmental feedback to the team regarding the output of its work, and have the team evaluate its own internal workings to address any potential problems early.

17. Evaluate the entire team initiative on a regular basis to determine the extent to which it has met its organizational goals. Be prepared to modify the initiative depending on the results.

18. Use technological advances for teams in a way that is compatible with their tasks.

Employee Readiness for Change

Myriad changes accompany organizational life these days; a team approach to work is only one of them. There are also changes in organizational size, structure, technology, and labor-management relations, to name a few. Organizations that do not prepare their employees to deal effectively with change in general are not likely to induce them to want to become part of a team. Change often arouses fear and apprehension in employees. Organizations are not doing as much as they should when it comes to planning how and when to introduce teams, or providing support for those employees who are averse to change. Employees need to know why they are moving to a team-based approach. They also need to know how the change will affect their lives in at least four critical ways: performance, pay, management relationships, and structural control. Other areas of work will be affected as well, but these are the four that must be addressed. With proper planning and adequate information, employees might be more likely to embrace teamwork.

Management Readiness for Change

Along with the rank and file, managers must recognize a new role for themselves in a team-based environment. Often any new employee initiative is won or lost on the shop floor, where the new policies and procedures are implemented by the line managers. Training the managers in their new roles and helping them to deal with team issues—before asking them to implement team initiatives—is far better than having them flounder or sabotage the initiative.

Redefinition of the Job

In almost all organizations, the notion of a static, prescribed, long-term job has gone the way of the dodo bird. Still, to be effective, employees need to know what the general expectations are for their role in the organization's overall strategy. Even if an organization can't promise secure employment or that job duties will remain constant over time, it *can* work on defining the boundaries within which an employee is expected to operate. These boundaries will be fairly permeable and also fairly wide. For example, a clerical worker may no longer just be expected to type, file, and answer the phone. Instead, a boundary condition of keeping current with new word processing packages will be more in line with the new role that person is expected to take on. Although some people like to operate in totally ambiguous and seemingly chaotic work environments, most of us like more stability; it can be provided by defining the boundaries for work and the performance expectations for the role.

Performance, Accountability, and Reward Systems

Although performance, accountability, and reward systems are ostensibly the most powerful ways to leverage team performance, they are also hard to cope with for several reasons. First, because the ramifications are near and dear to most employees' hearts, tinkering with these systems often causes great anxiety. Second, as noted earlier, these systems have been created and used for managing individual performance, not teams. Third, these systems are tied to other systems, such as pensions, which are highly individualized for obvious reasons. As a result, team performance management is like walking on eggshells.

Nevertheless, the issues must be dealt with. Examples have been provided of how to initiate team performance assessment. Assessments then need to be linked to team accountability and team rewards. Teams as entire units need to be clear about what the organization expects of them, and individuals within teams need to be told explicitly what aspects of the team's work they are accountable for. If expectations are clear, then managing the reward system becomes more systematic.

I suspect that the ways in which organizations manage their team reward systems will vary tremendously. During an employment interview, potential employees should be asking: Are teams espoused in the organization? How are the teams rewarded? How is each member's accountability handled? These are tough questions, but they need to be answered. Input from teams, managers, and personnel departments all must be taken into account when formulating responses to these questions.

Plans for team performance, accountability, and rewards—as well as their execution—will be watched carefully by employees. An organization's way of managing performance, accountability, and rewards can be one of the most powerful motivators for employees to become part of a team; conversely, it can provoke employees to undermine the entire team initiative.

Issues of Commitment

With the rise of teams, it is impossible not to notice that some team members become more committed to their teams than to the organization as a whole. Organizations need to be cognizant of this fact and manage it. To be sure, commitment to the team is highly desirable in order to build team efficacy. But there is a downside—the goals of the organization may become subordinate to the team's goals. To avoid this problem, organizations must ensure that teams always feel they are a part of the organization and appreciated by it.

Unfortunately, in many organizations, the most successful teams are also the ones most likely to engender a higher level of commitment to the team rather than the organization. To counterbalance these feelings of commitment, the organization needs to be very vocal and public in its praise of successful teams. Organizations also need to reward successful teams by taking steps such as providing them more autonomy, making them part of the business strategy process, and finding other ways to ensure that members feel part of the organization as a whole.

Appropriate Use of Technology

With the increasing pace of technological change in both hardware and software, employees can become overwhelmed when trying to keep pace. As advocated in Chapter Eleven, organizations should use technology as a tool to facilitate either more effective or more efficient work. It is not always wise to jump at the newest technological advancements. Instead, teams and organizations should think through the pros and cons of using a particular technology and specifically how the change will impact the teams' work.

Research Issues

Many of the issues that team researchers face now are similar to the ones that they have always faced. From the standpoint of someone who carries out and is always on the lookout for new research findings on teams, this is disquieting. This problem is part of a larger systemic issue that divides science and practice. Although academic institutions toil away on team research in an abstract and theoretical manner, practitioners who are actually trying to manage teams and the changes that accompany them will find that the writings of academicians are often too esoteric, too user-unfriendly, and simply not of much practical help.

Unfortunately, the way the academic performance system operates, researchers often are caught up in evaluating the impact of things that have already occurred, as opposed to leading in producing new knowledge that will assist organizations (Berwald, 1998). Thus, the nine research questions that follow are still very much on the table, despite nearly two decades of active research programs by dozens of researchers.

Question One: What Is the Appropriate Level of Analysis: Individual Team Members or Teams as a Unit?

The correct response is, "It depends." If the variables of interest are ones that encompass individual differences and how those differences will affect the team, then individual units of analysis are appropriate. If the variables of interest are to be generalized at the team level, then the team is the best choice. There is a third level not even usually discussed, which is the level of the team initiative. Research at this level would strive to answer the question, What has initiating a team-based personnel system done to the organization's performance?

Question Two: What Is the Best Way to Cope with the Dynamic Nature of Teams?

Teams develop and change as their members become more used to the team environment and as team membership shifts. The only way to deal with this issue from a research standpoint is to conduct longitudinal studies. However, doing so is very difficult for most researchers, as they need access to teams on a regular basis. Researchers also have to have the financial resources to collect data over extended periods of time and across multiple teams. Despite these costly concerns, longitudinal designs would be a worthwhile development; the research literature is still populated by too many laboratory studies that use student groups as participants, meet only once in an experimental setting, and work on a task that is not personally relevant.

Question Three: What Is the Best Strategy for Dealing with the Various Contexts in Which Teams Operate?

Active programs of research that provide instruments to collect this information across contexts are needed. Otherwise, the context is left as part of the error variance while the variables of interest to a particular researcher are examined more closely. More work on the contextual variables themselves—how they operate and why—needs to be conducted. These variables are critical in the performance of teams that actually exist within contexts.

Question Four: What Do We Mean by Team Processes, and How Do We Measure Them?

The definition of team processes has changed over the past two decades. Early on, team processes had more to do with personality clashes and team cohesiveness; more recently, process variables such as communication flow, information exchange, and linkages to leaders have played a more prominent role. As a result, researchers now have new constructs but they do not yet have enough concrete definitions or reliable and valid measuring tools to accompany them.

Question Five: What Do We Mean by Team Performance, and How Do We Measure It?

One can argue that this is the most critical issue for organizations to deal with. Researchers can go a long way in assisting organizations by providing them with tools by which to evaluate their teams. Organizations must also determine who is going to do the evaluating. I have advocated a multiple-source approach in this book, with team members, team coaches, team supervisors, and team customers to be used whenever possible. All of them have a role to play in assessing the overall effectiveness of the team.

Question Six: How Do We Best Integrate Results from Case Study and Quantitative Approaches?

Research that uses fine-grained case study approaches—with the goal of unique understanding—and research that uses cross-team quantitative approaches—with the goal of generalizability—is not easily integrated. This problem will continue as long as we have researchers using different approaches. Clearly the response to the question cannot be all or none. Fine-grained case studies provide a rich source of ideas about why teams succeed or fail; without them, researchers might cling to ideas from the past that might not even be relevant any more and miss the most salient variables affecting team performance. Studies of the cross-team type collect numerical data in different contexts; these provide a substantiating mechanism to determine whether those variables suggested by case studies actually are relevant for most teams, and if so, to what extent. Findings from both types of research need to be integrated as practitioners decide which variables are most likely to be relevant for teams in their organizations. Referring to both types of findings in literature searches and introductory sections of articles would go some way to alleviating the false dichotomy of the case study versus cross-team approaches.

Question Seven: What Does Team Leadership Mean?

There is very little to guide this research, as the general leadership literature is a far cry from being coherent in and of itself. My work suggests that there are obvious roles for the team leader to play. For instance, teams need an individual to run interference for them and to procure resources for them. They need an arbitrator to deal with dysfunctional members. They need someone to help them set goals that are consistent with the organization. In Chapter Four I identified the roles that team members want leaders to take on. There are other aspects to leadership than simply those that are role-defined which need closer scrutiny. Selecting team leaders, for instance, is an area that needs to be looked at more closely. Effective training tools for team leaders is another part of the team leadership puzzle that needs work.

Leadership, as I have used the term throughout this book, is position leadership. Leaders defined in this way are individuals who have power over teams by virtue of their positions in an organizational hierarchy. The issue of member leadership within the team itself is an altogether different issue, and one that needs to be addressed given the proliferation of self-directed work teams.

Question Eight: What Is the Contribution of Team Members' Knowledge, Skills, and Attitudes to Team Performance?

Measuring instruments to evaluate the knowledge, skills, and attitudes of team members are just now becoming available. It will be some time before the linkages between these variables and overall team performance is made concretely. It will be longer still before practitioners are told how to obtain the right mix of knowledge, skills, and attitudes for the task at hand.

Question Nine: Is There a Theoretical Framework to Assist in Making Sense of the Disparate Information We Have About Teams?

Right now the response is a resounding no! There are so many theories about team performance, there are so many variables involved, and there are so many different ways to measure those variables that we are a long way from having a comprehensive theory of team performance. Guzzo (1995b) reflected on this lack of coherence: "Rather than interpret the lack of unity in perspectives as incoherence and confusion, I shall suggest here that it indicates high-energy research and inquiry" (p. 393). If we take Guzzo's optimistic approach, then the search for common threads among the myriad studies published and books written on team performance will be worthwhile. Each perspective will provide some insight into how your team works in your organization. The search will provide ideas about variables you may not have thought of as being relevant.

Final Thoughts

I have provided one model of team performance as the organizing framework for this book. It reflects my biases based on what I have observed, what I have read, and what I have found in my own research and practice with teams. One of its strengths is its comprehensive inclusion of the variables involved. Another of its strengths is that it provides explicit ways for practitioners to use the material presented.

One's greatest strengths are always one's greatest weaknesses, however. Because the model is so complex and inclusive, I do not suggest that a single approach will make teams effective. Instead, readers need to go through each chapter to find the ideas that are most useful for them in their context with their own teams. I believe that the best way to help teams and team managers improve effectiveness is by providing them with a number of options. They know their teams far better than I ever could, and so they will find that some ideas resonate most strongly with their unique situations. Improving the odds for each team's effectiveness by providing a wide array of options and techniques was my purpose in writing this book in the first place.

REFERENCES

Auger, B. Y. *How to Run Better Business Meetings: A Businessman's Guide to Meetings That Get Things Done.* St. Paul, MN: 3M Company, Visual Products Division, 1972.

Baker, D. P., & Salas, E. "Principles for Measuring Teamwork: A Summary and Look Toward the Future." In M. T. Brannick, E. Salas, & C. Prince (Eds.), *Team Performance Assessment and Measurement* (pp. 331–355). Hillsdale, NJ: Erlbaum, 1997.

Baker, D. P., Salas, E., Campion, M. A., Cannon-Bowers, J., Higgs, A. C., & Levine, E. L. "Job Analysis for Teams: Fitting Square Pegs into Round Holes?" Panel discussion at the 13th annual conference of the Society for Industrial and Organizational Psychology, Dallas, TX, April 1998.

Bandura, A. *Self-Efficacy: The Exercise of Control.* New York: Freeman, 1977.

Bandura, A. *Social Foundations of Thought and Action: A Social-Cognitive View.* Englewood Cliffs, NJ: Prentice-Hall, 1986.

Bernardin, H. J., & Buckley, M. R. "Strategies in Rater Training." *Academy of Management Review, 6,* 205–212, 1981.

Berwald, M.C.A. "The Challenge of Profound Transformation for Industrial and Organizational Psychologists: Are We Meeting the Challenge?" *Canadian Psychology, 39,* 158–163, 1998.

Bies, R. J., & Shapiro, D. L. "Voice and Justification: Their Influence on Procedural Fairness Judgment." *Academy of Management Journal, 31,* 378–385, 1988.

Brannick, M. T., Salas, E., & Prince, C. (Eds.). *Team Performance Assessment and Measurement.* Hillsdale, NJ: Erlbaum, 1997.

Cannon-Bowers, J. A., Salas, E., & Blickensderfer, E. L. "Making Fine Distinctions Among Team Constructs: Worthy Endeavor or 'Crewel' and Unusual Punishment?" In R. Klimoski (Chair), *When Is a Work Team a Crew and Does It Matter?* Paper presented at the

13th annual conference of the Society for Industrial and Organizational Psychology, Dallas, TX, April 1998.

Cappelli, P., Bassi, L., Katz, H., Knoke, D., Osterman, P., & Useem, M. *Change at Work.* New York: Oxford University Press, 1997.

Carnes, W. T. *Effective Meetings for Busy People: Let's Decide It and Go Home.* New York: McGraw-Hill, 1980.

Cartwright, D., & Zander, A. W. (Eds.). *Group Dynamics: Research and Theory* (3rd ed.). New York: HarperCollins, 1967.

Cherrington, D. J., & England, J. L. "The Desire for an Enriched Job as a Moderator of the Enrichment-Satisfaction Relationship." *Organizational Behavior and Human Performance, 25,* 139–159, 1980.

Ciborra, C. U. *Groupware and Teamwork.* New York: Wiley, 1996.

Costa, P. T. Jr., & McCrea, R. R. *Revised NEO Personality Inventory and New Five-Factor Inventory* (professional manual). Odessa, FL: Psychological Assessment Resources, 1992.

Dickinson, T. L., & McIntyre, R. M. "A Conceptual Framework for Teamwork Measurement." In M. T. Brannick, E. Salas, & C. Prince (Eds.), *Team Performance Assessment and Measurement* (pp. 19–43). Hillsdale, NJ: Erlbaum, 1997.

Drucker, P. F. *Landmarks of Tomorrow: A Report on the New "Post-Modern" World.* New York: HarperCollins, 1959.

Eby, L. T., Meade, A., Parisi, A. G., Douthitt, S. S., & Midden, P. "Measuring Mental Models for Teamwork at the Individual and Team Level." Paper presented at the 13th annual conference of the Society for Industrial and Organizational Psychology, Dallas, TX, April 1998.

Einhorn, H. J., & McCoach, W. P. "A Simple Multiattribute Utility Procedure for Evaluation." *Behavioral Science, 22,* 270–282, 1977.

Fischer, G. W. "Multidimensional Utility Models for Risky and Riskless Choice." *Organizational Behavior and Human Performance, 17,* 127–146, 1976.

Gersick, C.J.G. "Time and Transitions in Work Teams: Toward a New Model of Group Development." *Academy of Management Journal, 31,* 9–41, 1988.

Gersick, C.J.G. "Marking Time: Predictable Transitions in Work Groups." *Academy of Management Journal, 32,* 274–309, 1989.

Gladstein, D. "Groups in Context: A Model of Task Group Effectiveness." *Administrative Science Quarterly, 29,* 499–517, 1984.

Goodman, P. S. "Impact of Task Technology on Group Performance." In P.S. Goodman & Associates (Eds.), *Designing Effective Work Groups* (pp. 120–167). San Francisco: Jossey-Bass, 1986.

Greenburg, S. "Computer-Supported Cooperative Work and Groupware: An Introduction to the Special Issue." *International Journal of Man-Machine Studies, 34,* 133–141, 1991.

Grudin, J. "History and Focus." *Institute of Electrical and Electronics Engineers,* 19–26, May 1994.

Guzzo, R. A. "Introduction: At the Intersection of Team Effectiveness and Decision Making." In R. A. Guzzo, E. Salas, & Associates (Eds.), *Team Effectiveness and Decision Making in Organizations* (pp. 1–8). San Francisco: Jossey-Bass, 1995a.

Guzzo, R. A. "Conclusion: Common Themes Among the Diversity." In R.A. Guzzo, E. Salas, & Associates (Eds.), *Team Effectiveness and Decision Making in Organizations* (pp. 381–394). San Francisco: Jossey-Bass, 1995b.

Guzzo, R. A., & Shea, G. P. "Group Performance and Intergroup Relations in Organizations." In M. D. Dunnette & L. M. Hough (Eds.), *Handbook of Industrial & Organizational Psychology* (2nd ed., Vol. 3, pp. 269–313). Palo Alto, CA: Consulting Psychologists Press, 1992.

Guzzo, R. A., Yost, P. R., Campbell, R. J., & Shea, G. P. "Potency in Groups: Articulating a Construct." *British Journal of Social Psychology, 32*, 87–106, 1993.

Hackman, J. R. "The Design of Work Teams." In J. W. Lorsch (Ed.), *Handbook of Organizational Behavior* (pp. 315–342). Englewood Cliffs, NJ: Prentice-Hall, 1987.

Hackman, J. R. *Groups That Work (and Those That Don't): Creating Conditions for Effective Teamwork.* San Francisco: Jossey-Bass, 1990.

Hackman, J. R., & Oldham, G. R. *Work Redesign.* Reading, MA: Addison-Wesley, 1980.

Hallam, G., & Campbell, D. "The Measurement of Team Performance with a Standardized Survey." In M. T. Brannick, E. Salas, & C. Prince (Eds). *Team Performance Assessment and Measurement* (pp. 155–171). Hillsdale, NJ: Erlbaum, 1997.

Hickson, D. J., Pugh, D. S., & Pheysey, D. C. "Operations Technology and Organization Structure: An Empirical Reappraisal." *Administrative Science Quarterly, 14*, 378–397, 1969.

Hildebrand, C. "A Little of That Human Touch." *Chief Information Officer, 9*, 64–70, 1996.

Hollingshead, A. B., & McGrath, J. E. "Computer-Assisted Groups: A Critical Review of the Empirical Research." In R. A. Guzzo, E. Salas, & Associates (Eds.), *Team Effectiveness and Decision Making in Organizations* (pp. 46–78). San Francisco: Jossey-Bass, 1995.

Hogan, R. T. "Personality and Personality Measurement." In M. D. Dunnette & L. M. Hough (Eds.), *Handbook of Industrial & Organizational Psychology* (2nd ed., Vol. 2, pp. 873–919). Palo Alto, CA: Consulting Psychologists Press, 1992.

Huber, G. P. *Managerial Decision Making.* Glenview, IL: Scott, Foresman, 1980.

Jackson, S. E., May, K. E., & Whitney, K. "Understanding the Dynamics of Diversity in Decision-Making Teams." In R. A. Guzzo, E. Salas (Eds.), & Associates, *Team Effectiveness and Decision Making in Organizations* (pp. 204–261). San Francisco: Jossey-Bass, 1995.

Janis, I. *Groupthink* (2nd ed.). Boston: Houghton Mifflin, 1982.

Jessup, H. R. "New Roles in Team Leadership." *Training and Development Journal*, 79–83, November 1990.

Johnson, D. W., & Johnson, R. "Social Interdependence and Perceived Academic and Personal Support in the Classroom." *Journal of Social Psychology, 120*, 77–82, 1983.

Johnson, D. W., Johnson, R., & Anderson, D. "Social Interdependence and Classroom Climate." *Journal of Psychology, 114*, 135–142, 1983.

Kanter, R. M. *When Giants Learn to Dance: Mastering Strategy, Management, and Careers in the 1990s.* New York: Simon & Schuster, 1989.

Keeney, R. L., & Raiffa, H. *Decisions with Multiple Objectives: Preferences and Value Trade-Offs.* New York: Wiley, 1976.

Kichuk, S. L., & Weisner, W. H. "Work Teams: Selecting Members for Optimal Performance." *Canadian Psychology, 39*, 23–32, 1998.

King, W. R. "Strategic Issues in Groupware." *Information Systems Management, 2*, 73–75, 1996.

Kline, T.J.B. "Cooperativeness and Competitiveness: Dimensionality and Gender-Specificity." *Educational and Psychological Measurement, 55*, 335–339, 1995.

Kline, T.J.B. *Predicting Team Performance: A Field Study.* Unpublished manuscript (currently under review), 1999a.

Kline, T.J.B. "The Team Player Inventory: Reliability and Validity of a Measure of Predisposition Towards Organizational Team Working Environments." *Journal for Specialists in Group Work, 24*, 102–112, 1999b.

Kline, T.J.B., & Gardiner, H. "The Successful Adoption of Groupware: Perceptions of the Users." *Human Systems Management, 16*, 301–306, 1997.

Kline, T.J.B., & MacLeod, M. "Predicting Organizational Team Performance." *Organization Development Journal, 15*, 77–84, 1997.

Kline, T.J.B., MacLeod, M., & McGrath, J. "Team Effectiveness: Contributors and Hindrances." *Human Systems Management, 15,* 183–186, 1996.

Kline, T.J.B., & McGrath, J. "Development and Validation of Five Criteria for Evaluating Team Performance." *Organization Development Journal, 16,* 19–27, 1998.

Kline, T.J.B., & McGrath, J. "A Review of the Groupware Literature: Theories, Methodologies, and a Research Agenda." *Canadian Psychology,* forthcoming.

Kline, T.J.B., & Sell, Y. P. "Cooperativeness vs. Competitiveness: Initial Findings Regarding Effects on the Performance of Individual and Group Problem-Solving." *Psychological Reports, 79,* 355–365, 1996.

Kraiger, K., & Wenzel, L. H. "Conceptual Development and Empirical Evaluation of Measures of Shared Mental Models as Indicators of Team Effectiveness." In M. T. Brannick, E. Salas, & C. Prince (Eds.), *Team Performance Assessment and Measurement* (pp. 63–84). Hillsdale, NJ: Erlbaum, 1997.

Krasner, H., McInroy, J., & Walz, D. B. "Groupware Research and Technology Issues with Application to Software Process Management." *IEEE Transactions on Systems, Man, and Cybernetics, 21,* 704–712, 1991.

Lawler, E. E. III, & Mohrman, S. A. "Quality Circles: After the Honeymoon." *Organizational Dynamics,* 42–55, Spring 1987.

Leavitt, H. "Suppose We Took Groups Seriously. . . ." In E. L. Class & F. G. Zimmer (Eds.), *Man and Work in Society* (pp. 67–77). New York: Van Nostrand Reinhold, 1975.

Lindsley, D. H., Brass, D. J., & Thomas, J. B. "Efficacy-Performance Spirals: A Multilevel Perspective." *Academy of Management Review, 20,* 645–678, 1995.

Locke, E. A., & Latham, G. P. *A Theory of Goal Setting and Task Performance.* Englewood Cliffs, NJ: Prentice-Hall, 1990.

Luft, J., Kingsbury, S., & Schrader, H. "Shared Concerns: Psychometrics in Human Interaction." *NTL News & Views,* 10–12, April 1990.

Manz, C. C., & Simms, H. P. *Superleadership: Leading Others to Lead Themselves.* Englewood Cliffs, NJ: Prentice-Hall, 1989.

Mayo, E. *The Human Problems of an Industrial Civilization.* New York: Macmillan, 1933.

McClough, A. C., & Rogelberg, S. G. "An Exploration of Stevens and Campion's Teamwork Knowledge, Skill, and Ability Instrument." Paper presented at the 13th annual conference of the Society for Industrial and Organizational Psychology, Dallas, TX, April 1998.

McGrath, J. E. "Studying Groups at Work: Ten Critical Needs for Theory and Practice." In P. S. Goodman & Associates (Eds.), *Designing Effective Work Groups* (pp. 362–391). San Francisco: Jossey-Bass, 1986.

McGrath, J. E., & Altman, I. *Small Group Research: A Synthesis and Critique of the Field.* Austin, TX: Holt, Rinehart and Winston, 1966.

McGrath, J. E., Berdahl, J. L., & Arrow, H. "Traits, Expectations, Culture, and Clout: Dynamics of Diversity in Workgroups." In S. E. Jackson & M. N. Ruderman (Eds.), *Diversity in Work Teams: Research Paradigms for a Changing Workplace* (pp. 17–45). Washington, D.C.: American Psychological Association, 1995.

Methot, L. L., & Phillips-Grant, K. "Technological Advances in the Canadian Workplace: An I-O Perspective." *Canadian Psychology, 39,* 133–141, 1998.

Morhman, S. A., Cohen, S. G., & Mohrman, A. M., Jr. *Designing Team-Based Organizations: New Forms for Knowledge Work.* San Francisco: Jossey-Bass, 1995.

Morgan, B. B. Jr., Glickman, A. S., Woodward, E. A., Blaiwes, A. S., & Salas, E. *Measurement of Teams Behaviors in a Navy Environment* (NTSC Tech. Rep. No. TR–86–014). Orlando, FL: Naval Training Systems Center, 1986.

Morgan, G. *Images of Organization* (2nd ed.). Thousand Oaks, CA: Sage, 1997.

Nadler, D. A., & Ancona, D. "Teamwork at the Top: Creating Executive Teams That Work." In D. A. Nadler, M. S. Gertstein, & R. B. Shaw (Eds.), *Organizational Architecture: Designs for Changing Organizations* (pp. 209–231). San Francisco: Jossey-Bass, 1992.

Nieva, V. F., Fleishman, E. A., & Reick, A. *Team Dimensions: Their Identity, Their Measurement, and Their Relationships* (Final Tech. Rep. for Contract No. DAHC 19–78–C–0001). Washington DC: Advanced Research Resources Organization, 1978.

Noonan, L. "Impact of Frame-of-Reference and Behavioural Observation Training on Rating and Behavioural Accuracy in Performance Appraisals." Unpublished master's thesis, University of Calgary, Alberta, Canada, 1996.

Nurick, A. "Participating in Organizational Change: A Longitudinal Field Study." *Human Relations, 35*, 413–430, 1982.

Oldham, G. R., Hackman, J. R., & Pearce, J. L. "Conditions Under Which Employees Respond Positively to Enriched Work." *Journal of Applied Psychology, 61*, 395–403, 1976.

Osterman, P. "How Common Is Workplace Transformation and How Can We Explain Who Does It?" *Industrial and Labor Relations Review, 12*, 173–188, 1994.

Parker, G. M. *Team Players and Teamwork.* San Francisco: Jossey-Bass, 1996.

Perrow, C. "A Framework for the Comparative Analysis of Organizations." *American Sociological Review, 32*, 194–208, 1967.

Peters, T. J., & Waterman, R. H. *In Search of Excellence: Lessons from America's Best-Run Companies.* New York: HarperCollins, 1982.

Pulakos, E. D. "A Comparison of Rater Training Programs: Error Training and Accuracy Training." *Journal of Applied Psychology, 69*, 581–588, 1984.

Pulakos, E. D. "The Development of Training Programs to Increase Accuracy with Different Rating Tasks." *Organizational Behavior and Human Decision Processes, 38*, 78–91, 1989.

Reddy, W. B. *Intervention Skills: Process Consultation for Small Groups and Teams.* San Diego: Pfeiffer, 1994.

Roethlisberger, F. J., & Dickson, W. J. *Management and the Worker.* Cambridge, MA: Harvard University Press, 1939.

Schein, E. S. "Organizational Culture." *American Psychologist, 45*, 109–119, 1990.

Shea, G. P., & Guzzo, R. A. "Group Effectiveness: What Really Matters?" *Sloan Management Review, 28*, 25–31, 1987a.

Shea, G. P., & Guzzo, R. A. "Groups as Human Resources." In K. M. Rowland & G. R. Ferris (Eds.), *Research in Personnel and Human Resources Management* (Vol. 5, pp. 323–356). Greenwich, CT: JAI Press, 1987b.

Steiner, I. D. *Group Processes and Productivity.* New York: Academic Press, 1972.

Sulsky, L. M., & Day, D. V. "Frame-of-Reference Training and Cognitive Categorization: An Empirical Investigation of Rater Memory Issues." *Journal of Applied Psychology, 77*, 501–510, 1992.

Sundstrom, E., DeMeuse, K. P., Futrell, D. "Work Teams: Applications and Effectiveness." *American Psychologist, 45*, 120–133, 1990.

Thompson, J. D. *Organizations in Action.* New York: McGraw-Hill, 1967.

Thornton, C., & Lockhart, E. "Groupware or Electronic Brainstorming." *Journal of Systems Management, 10*, 10–12, 1994.

Tiegs, R. B., Tetrick, L. E., & Fried, Y. "Growth Need Strength and Context Satisfactions as Moderators of the Relations of the Job Characteristics Model." *Journal of Management, 18*, 575–593, 1992.

Tjosvold, D. *Working Together to Get Things Done: Managing for Organizational Productivity.* San Francisco: New Lexington Press, 1986.

Townsend, A. M., DeMarie, S., & Hendrickson, A. R. "Virtual Teams: Technology and the Workplace of the Future." *Academy of Management Executive, 12,* 17–29, 1998.

Trist, E. L. *The Evolution of Sociotechnical Systems: A Conceptual Framework and an Action Research Program.* Toronto, Ontario: Ontario Quality of Working Life Centre, 1981.

Tropman, J. E. *Making Meetings Work.* Thousand Oaks, CA: Sage, 1996.

Tropman, J. E., & Morningstar, G. *Meetings: How to Make Them Work for You.* New York: Van Nostrand Reinhold, 1985.

Tuckman, B. W. "Developmental Sequence in Small Groups." *Psychological Bulletin, 63,* 384–399, 1965.

Valacich, J. S., Dennis, A. R., & Nunamaker, J. F. Jr. "Electronic Meeting Support: The Group Systems Concept." *International Journal of Man-Machine Studies, 34,* 261–282, 1991.

Varney, G. H. *Building Productive Teams: An Action Guide and Resource Book.* San Francisco: Jossey-Bass, 1989.

Watson, W., Michaelson, L. K., & Sharp, W. "Member Competence, Group Interaction, and Group Decision Making: A Longitudinal Study." *Journal of Applied Psychology, 76,* 803–809, 1991.

Webber, S. S. "Distinguishing Crews from Teams: An Empirical Investigation." In R. Klimoski (Chair), *When Is a Work Team a Crew and Does It Matter?* Symposium presented at the 13th annual conference of the Society for Industrial and Organizational Psychology, Dallas, TX, April 1998.

Welbourne, T. M., Johnson, D. E., & Erez, A. "The Role-Based Performance Scale: Validity Analysis of a Theory-Based Measure." *Academy of Management Journal, 41,* 540–555, 1998.

Wellins, R. S., Byham, W. C., & Wilson, J. M. *Empowered Teams: Creating Self-Directed Work Groups That Improve Quality, Productivity, and Participation.* San Francisco: Jossey-Bass, 1991.

West, M. "Team Research: Methodology and Measurement Challenges." Panel discussion at the 13th annual conference of the Society for Industrial and Organizational Psychology, Dallas, TX, April 1998.

Witteman, H. "Group Member Satisfaction: A Conflict-Related Account." *Small Group Research, 22,* 24–58, 1991.

Woodward, J. *Industrial Organization: Theory and Practice.* London: Oxford University Press, 1965.

Yeatts, D. E., & Hyten, C. *High-Performing Self-Managed Work Teams: A Comparison of Theory to Practice.* Thousand Oaks, CA: Sage, 1998.

Zander, A. W., & Medow, H. "Individual and Group Levels of Aspiration." *Human Relations, 16,* 89–105, 1963.

Zander, A. W., & Newcomb, T. "Group Levels of Aspiration in United Fund Campaigns." *Journal of Personality and Social Psychology, 9,* 157–162, 1967.

INDEX

HOW TO USE THE DISK

The minimum configuration needed to utilize the files included on this disk is a computer system with one 3.5" floppy disk drive capable of reading double-sided high-density IBM formatted floppy disks and word processing or desktop publishing software able to read Microsoft WORD 6.0/95 files. Document memory needs will vary, but your system should be capable of opening file sizes of 80+K. No monitor requirements other than the ones established by your document software need be met.

Each of the exhibits and case studies in your textbook that are marked with a disk icon have a corresponding team exercise that has been saved onto the enclosed disk as a Microsoft WORD 6.0/95 file. These files can be opened with many Windows- and Macintosh-based word processors or desktop publishers for viewing or editing as you see fit. The files were originally created and saved as a WORD 6.0/95 DOC file by Microsoft Word 97. Not all software will read the files exactly the same, but the DOC format is an honest attempt by Jossey-Bass/Pfeiffer Publishers to preserve the composition of the figures such as borders, fonts, character attributes, bullets, etc., as accurately as possible.

Copy all DOC files to a directory/folder in your computer system. To read the files using your Windows-based document software, select File from the main menu followed by Open to display the Open dialog box. Set the correct drive letter and subdirectory shown in the Open dialog box by using the Look in control. In the Files of type text box enter *.doc to display the list of DOC files available in the subdirectory.

Each file name is coded to its exhibit or case study in the text to make it easy for you to find the one you want. For example, Exercise Form 3.1 has been named EXR03-01.DOC. You can open the file by either double-clicking your mouse on the file name that you want to open or by clicking once on the file name to select it and then once on the Open command button.